W9-BBA-160

RELIGION AND PEACE

KANSAS SCHOOL OF RELIGION
University of Kansas
1300 Oread Avenue
LAWRENCE, KANSAS 66044

RELIGION
AND
PEACE

Papers from the
National Inter-Religious Conference on Peace

edited by
HOMER A. JACK

The Bobbs-Merrill Company, Inc.
A Subsidiary of Howard W. Sams & Co., Inc.
Publishers   Indianapolis   New York   Kansas City

CONTENTS

PREFACE

Organized religion throughout history has been generally concerned with the institution of war. Sometimes church and synagogue have actually blessed war, and occasionally they have opposed it. Between the two world wars in the twentieth century, and
partly as a result of the social gospel movement, American clergymen and laymen tried to establish new relationships between religion and international relations. A religious peace movement—
including pacifism—that developed, however, did not officially
encompass church and synagogue. Most religious institutions in
the world supported their nations' efforts in World Wars I and II.
With the incidence of mass killing by so-called conventional
weapons, and with the advent of atomic warfare, the line between
pacifism and non-pacifism became blurred as all churchmen had to
grapple with new theological and moral issues. This has been, in
greatest measure, on a denominational level, because the larger co-
ordinating groups have not been assigned responsibility to make
new statements.

Since World War II, many of the religious groups in the West
have made their own studies and pronouncements in the field of
war and foreign policy. The World Council of Churches, since its
establishment in 1948, has issued many statements through its
Commission of the Churches on International Affairs. The National Council of Churches of Christ in the United States has ex-

plored certain international issues thoroughly, especially through its World Order Study Conferences, the sixth of which was held in St. Louis in October 1965. Individual Protestant denominations have increasingly issued sophisticated pronouncements; while in the Roman Catholic Church, most dramatically, the church's position in regard to war was given prominence with the issuing of the *Pacem in Terris* encyclical by the late Pope John XXIII in April 1963. Schema XIII, debated by Vatican Council II in the autumn of 1965, constitutes a definitive position for the Catholic Church on this issue. The various Jewish bodies have brought traditional prophecy up to date through statements of the rabbinate and conferences of laymen and rabbis.

However, despite these separate statements, often the result of national and even international meetings, there has been little inter-religious confrontation on these issues. The Council of Religion and International Affairs (formerly the Church Peace Union) has published significant material and sponsored small inter-religious dialogues, and then on selected issues. The Church Peace Mission works predominantly among Protestants, while the Fellowship of Reconciliation and its affiliated denominational peace fellowships have only begun to bring non-Protestants into their conferences. The Catholic Association for International Peace has been in operation for many years, while the conference on "Jewish Dimensions in Peace" was a new initiative. The *Pacem in Terris* convocation of February 1965 was the most dramatic peace conference ever held in America, but its origin was almost wholly secular. The Christian Peace Conference, with headquarters in Prague, has held two international meetings and may be growing beyond its Protestant and Eastern European origins. Several world conferences on peace and religion have been organized in Japan, but their value has chiefly been to involve non-Western religions.

Feeling the need for increased inter-religious dialogue on peace, Rabbi Maurice Eisendrath, of the Union of American Hebrew Congregations, and Dr. Dana McLean Greeley, of the Unitarian Universalist Association, independently conceived the possibility of convening an American and then an international conference on religion and peace. They joined with Roman Catholic Bishop John J. Wright of Pittsburgh, Methodist Bishop John

Wesley Lord of Washington, Episcopal Bishop Daniel J. Corrigan of New York, and many others to plan an exploratory Religious Leaders' Conference on Peace. This was held at the Church Center for the United Nations in mid-January 1965. Out of this successful gathering came the call for the National Inter-Religious Conference on Peace.

The purpose of the National Conference was fourfold: (1) to bring together clergymen and laymen from all peace-oriented viewpoints to discuss the relation of religion to peace; (2) to analyze in depth the basic religious statements on war and peace and on the moral principles in world order, to find parallel moral principles and to seek approximate guidelines; (3) to discuss current problems from the viewpoint of these principles and proximate norms; (4) to analyze existing religious programs in Washington, at the U. N., on the local level, and in the world community, and to recommend further co-operation so that organized religion can play its role in governmental decisions affecting war and peace.

The conference was held on March 15–17, 1966, in Washington, D.C., and was attended by almost five hundred clergymen and laymen. At its conclusion, participants voted that this inter-religious dialogue extend in three directions: (1) the convening of a World Inter-Religious Conference on Peace, encompassing participation of all the world's religious traditions; (2) the calling of a National Conference on Religion and Peace, jointly with the Synagogue Council of America, the National Council of Churches, the National Catholic Welfare Conference, and other religious bodies; and (3) the urging of all religious, inter-religious, and community groups to intensify their work for peace, including the convening of regional and local inter-religious conferences.

We feel that the level of inter-religious thought, action, and commitment for peace in the United States was raised because of this conference. We hope, with God's will, that it will be extended ever higher in the future.

> Rabbi Maurice N. Eisendrath
> Dr. Dana McLean Greeley
> Bishop John E. Hines
> Archbishop Iakovos
> Bishop John Wesley Lord
> Bishop John J. Wright

INTRODUCTION

In the past decade there have been a number of discussions and conferences by representatives of organized religion on particular problems of war and peace. Yet probably never before has there been such an inclusive "mix" of organized religion and peace as in the National Inter-Religious Conference on Peace.

The results of this conference exceeded the less than modest hopes of its sponsors, although the initial fears were many. Could religious pacifists and non-pacifists find common ground for agreement, or would a conference only re-echo the rugged debates of the late 1930's? Could religious activists and other religious leaders meet in harmony or would a conference reveal a continuing division between market place and ivory tower? Could members of the several denominations and faiths, with varying history, theology, polity, and constituency, work together satisfactorily, or would a conference only gloss over irreconcilable differences?

During the more than three years that the co-chairmen and the executive committee worked in preparing this conference, a number of events occurred which substantially eased their task. For one thing, the dream of ecumenicity was rapidly becoming a fact, through the work of Vatican Council II, the World Council of Churches, and other groups. Also, some of the inhibitions of organized Protestantism in the war/peace field gave way as the leaders of the National Council of Churches saw the spectacular results of their free-wheeling Commission on Religion and Race and resolved to inaugurate a new if not identical program in peace. The realities of the nuclear age have increasingly blurred some of the previous divisions between pacifists and non-pacifists. The escalating war in Vietnam during 1965–66 also made many church-men who participated in Selma-like demonstrations for greater civil rights transfer their experience more quickly into actions for peace. Thus "new faces" appeared in the National Emergency Committee of Clergy Concerned About Vietnam.

In this new atmosphere, the conference evolved with fewer problems than anticipated. The only false start was an early at-tempt to liken the National Conference of 1966 in Washington to the National Conference on Religion and Race of 1963 in Chicago. When some of the so-called umbrella religious organizations found it difficult to co-operate officially with the conference, it was agreed not to press the parallel. Thus the conference was com-pletely unofficial, sponsored only by the six co-chairmen and other prominent leaders of church and synagogue, but not by any de-nomination or council. Actually, some religious groups became supporting organizations, many contributing toward the financial costs. The total budget of the conference, including the mainte-nance of a small office in Washington, was less than $20,000—a figure that in no way indicates the amount of time and effort con-tributed by the co-chairmen and other members of the executive committee and especially by the so-called secretariat, the latter composed of denominational executives working full time in the field of international relations.

In preparation for the conference, several of the co-chairmen held a meeting with U. N. Secretary General U Thant, who gave the project every encouragement. He was unable to speak to the conference, but sent a warm message of greeting. The President of the United States was likewise unable to attend, but he sent a statement with his assistant, the Honorable Brooks Hays.

This was conceived as a working conference, and formal speeches were kept at a minimum. The two keynote addresses were given by Jewish and Protestant leaders, and the closing address by a leading Catholic prelate. Speeches were also given by Vice Presi-dent Hubert H. Humphrey and by Arthur W. Barber of the Department of Defense. The conference, wishing to obtain the best thinking of administration officials without being bound by them, also welcomed discussants from the Department of State. There was also a noon-time panel composed of representatives of the religious press, viewing the work of organized religion for peace.

The three workshops were held concurrently—for a total of eleven hours each—and participants generally stayed with the workshop of their choice. They received in advance a conference kit containing statements of the various religious groups on international relations, background materials for the particular workshop, and the specifically prepared position paper. The task of the workshop was to prepare a report on the subject matter using the position paper as a base but not being confined to it. As a matter of fact, the first two workshops modified their position papers only slightly in their final reports to be received by the plenary of the conference. By consensus, two thirds of the participants in each workshop had to agree to each paragraph or idea for it to be included in the final report. The working paper for the third workshop was more controversial, and a new draft was approved only after an extraordinary session lasting from 11 p. m. to 2 a. m.

A conference subcommittee submitted a conference Declaration which was approved by the three-quarters majority agreed to in advance by the executive committee. One item of this report, submitted from the floor of the final plenary session, was included by a one-vote margin—beyond the three-quarters minimum. The subcommittee was chaired by Episcopal Bishop William Crittenden and included Governor Harold E. Stassen, Sister Thomasine, and Albert Vorspan.

The flavor of this working conference was reflected by the stature of the 450 religious leaders present—active churchmen who blocked out three days of their busy schedules and were present throughout. Key clergy and laymen participated fully. Women were also active, including some nuns, and young people were especially invited from church and synagogue groups. The interreligious quality of the conference was nowhere better exemplified than at the St. Patrick's Day breakfast given by Bishop Wright for the executive committee. It was said that kosher food was served and the Bishop wore a bright green yarmulke for the occasion.

Public interest in the conference was revealed by the presence of a large press contingent and by daily stories, even with competition from two aloft astronauts. The national Episcopal radio office taped the entire proceedings and an edited program was widely broadcast, while the American Broadcasting Company devoted a TV special to the conference. This volume is but another effort to widen still further the influence of this conference.

Conference Achievements

1) The conference succeeded in providing a rich, uninhibited, mature dialogue on some of the prime questions of our time: communism, China, and intervention.

2) The conference Declaration provided a series of substantive recommendations for effecting peace in Vietnam, which were endorsed by a large majority of participants. The experience of working together, often eighteen hours a day, showed that several of the previous rigidities have been relaxed and that great areas of consensus are possible.

3) Three workshop reports were prepared and received for study. These were not approved by the plenary, although the action recommendations were adopted for implementation. These reports compare favorably with other such statements of policy from governmental and non-governmental groups.

4) An indirect achievement was that the publicity about an *inter-religious* conference on peace raised hopes, not only among members of various denominations and faiths, but also among the general public. Many were inspired that church and synagogue could unite, however unofficially, to think through some of the deeply ethical problems of our times, ones that cannot be left solely to governments.

5) Goals to be reached in the future include: (1) the convening of a broader, more official National Conference on Religion and Peace; (2) the encouragement of smaller inter-religious conferences on peace in local communities; and (3) the creation of an exploratory world inter-religious symposium on peace.

Continuous Problems

It would be unfair not to mention problems the conference uncovered. Some churchmen find dealing with war/peace issues very new; some approach these issues with more conservative, certainly more tentative, presuppositions than others. At times there were deep divisions among participants, though not usually denominational. Often there was as wide a spread in viewpoints within the various denominations as among them.

Some churchmen still feel that church and synagogue have nothing special to say with respect to the complex problems of war and peace. It is true that church and synagogue may be only slowly developing experts who are equipped by education and experience with specialized knowledge in these fields. Yet some such experts were present at the conference and made valuable contributions.

A third problem is that some churchmen still resist attendance at such gatherings. The evangelicals, for example, though invited, were not present. Any future world symposium must achieve better Judaeo-Christian representation, quite apart from that of non-Western faiths.

One of the stark evidences of American efficiency is the speed with which a great convention hotel takes any group in its stride. The conference adjourned at 2:30 p.m., and within two hours a national square dance convention took over the hotel completely. The halls that had echoed with political debate and theological overtones were now filled with the music and movements of the new conventioneers. And the latter wore as distinctive garb as some of the clerics had done only a few hours before.

Ours is a culture where a religious conference is no longer held in a church or synagogue and where a square dance is no longer held in a country barn. One of the departing clerics asked of the arriving dancers: "Why are you coming to this convention?" The answer: "Because it's fun—and why did you attend your conference?" Answer: "Survival!" It is never that simple. Religious folk have as mixed motives as dancing folk. Is fun less of a religious pursuit than human survival? No doubt the hotel manager rated both conferences equally. Who is to judge—and by what standards?

A Volunteer Conference

The planning of this conference was a difficult task spanning several years. A small committee first met in 1963, comprised of

Rabbi Maurice Eisendrath, Dr. Dana McLean Greeley, Bishop
John Wesley Lord, Bishop John J. Wright, and some of their respective associates, among them Rabbi Balfour Brickner, Mr. Herman Will, Jr., Msgr. Edward G. Murray, and the editor. To
this initial group others were added, such as Bishop Daniel Corrigan. In January 1965 an exploratory conference was held at
the Church Center for the United Nations.

Soon thereafter the organizational form for the conference
was conceived. In addition to Rabbi Eisendrath, Dr. Greeley,
Bishop Lord, and Bishop Wright, Bishop John Hines, of the
Episcopal Church, and Archbishop Iakovos, of the Greek Ortho-
dox Church, agreed to be conference co-chairmen, with Msgr.
Edward G. Murray continuing as secretary-treasurer. An execu-
tive committee was formed, including Reverend Jacob B. Agus,
Dr. Norman Baugher, Mrs. John C. Bennett, Dr. Eugene Carson
Blake, Robert D. Bulkley, Miss Jane Evans, Dr. Robert Fang-
meier, Rabbi Arthur Gilbert, Mr. George Hardin, Mr. Alfred
Hassler, Dr. Arthur N. Holcombe, Mr. Robert Kopka, Monsignor
Francis J. Lally, Mr. Stewart Meacham, Rabbi David H. Panitz,
Dr. Paul Peachey, Rabbi Michael A. Robinson, Dr. W. Harold
Row, Dr. Howard Schomer, and former Governor Harold E.
Stassen.

A secretariat was additionally established, consisting princi-
pally of denominational executives with special responsibilities in
the field of international relations: Rabbi Balfour Brickner,
Reverend Leonidas C. Contos, Reverend Clifford Earle, Reverend
John H. Eberly, Mr. James Finn, Dr. Alan F. Geyer, Reverend
Herschel Halbert, Mr. Herman Will, Jr., Dr. E. Raymond Wilson,
and the editor.

The secretariat met every two or three weeks, in Washington
or New York. Six months before the conference was held, an office
was established in Washington, capably headed by Mrs. Kay
Shannon, administrative secretary. In addition, a number of persons agreed to write position papers, while others agreed to be
chairmen and secretaries of the three workshops. Another group
agreed to be discussants. Their names are given in the appropriate
places in this volume. All deserve repeated thanks for their untiring
efforts in the search for peace.

HOMER A. JACK

1

MESSAGES BY
U THANT
AND
LYNDON B. JOHNSON

THE UNITED NATIONS

I am very glad to know that there will be a National Inter-Religious Conference on Peace next week in Washington, D.C. I am equally glad that so many distinguished representatives of different faiths will be participating.

It is wholly appropriate that devout men of goodwill should join in the search for peace at the present time. This search transcends religious differences, for peace and the brotherhood of man are among the basic tenets of all religions.

Today there are many danger spots where serious conflicts are raging. In our interdependent world, it would be a mistake to think that such local or regional conflicts can be contained, as they can easily escalate and get out of hand. It is, therefore, the prime concern of people of all religions that they co-operate and work together in order to help reduce tensions and settle those disputes that threaten peace. It is only by so doing that we can realize the determination of the United Nations to save succeeding generations from the scourge of war.

U THANT
Secretary General

March 7, 1966

1

The best minds and the best men are stirred by the grave challenges to peace in our time.

I applaud the timely concern that prompted this National Inter-Religious Conference on Peace, and I welcome your participants to our nation's capital.

The billions we appropriate to conquer poverty will be worth little unless we vanquish the most crippling poverty—man's insufficiency of understanding, his meagerness of spirit.

The dollars we spend to eradicate disease will be wasted unless we isolate and control the deadliest of microbes—man's capacity for hatred, his penchant for violence.

We will gain little by merely talking of the "search for peace" or the "pursuit of peace," for peace cannot be found or captured, it must be built—and the building must be the work of many men.

The builders, honest men, may often differ. But we will be strong enough to profit by our differences if we are wise enough to remember the faith and the goals we share.

The building will be a long and difficult job. Today's world is a cauldron which at any moment could boil over into catastrophe. But living in such a world has taught us that our only victories will be won, not by putting more weapons in men's hands, but by putting more wisdom in their hearts.

As you seek to advance such wisdom, no one watches you with deeper interest—or higher hopes—than your President. I send you my greetings and good wishes.

LYNDON B. JOHNSON

March 15, 1966

2

The Conference Declaration*

The National Inter-Religious Conference on Peace, assembled in Washington, D.C., is testimony to a shared conviction that different religious traditions are mutually supportive in their efforts to help people find solutions to the issues of war and peace. The conference speaks for itself. It addresses this declaration to organized religion everywhere as well as to the general community and our government.

The Religious and Moral Imperatives

Foremost is our concern that much of the discussion involving our nation's posture on foreign policy and especially on the war in Vietnam has taken place without serious probing of the religious and moral issues involved. Members of the religious community too often seem to accept the world's belief that naked power reacting to threat, real or imagined, is all that really counts in the modern world. Our religious profession, however, does obligate us to proclaim the moral and religious dimensions in all relationships between all peoples and governments. We are called to repentance, forgiveness, and compassion, to faith and hope, to

* Approved by the final plenary session.

working for justice, to love against hate, to the task of peace-building rather than war-making. We recognize the claims of God and His covenants with men in fulfilling His purposes in history. We cannot leave to soldiers and statesmen alone the great problems of conscience being raised in these days of conflict.

General Areas of Concern

Our discussion involved, first, confronting the changing Communist world. Changes in today's world may be seen, in part, as manifestations of Divine judgment to which we of the religious communities are challenged to respond in new ways. Our task is to press for peaceful solutions of conflicts between the United States and Communist governments which will respect the legitimate national interests of all parties. We believe our unique contribution can be expressed through personal contacts and intensive dialogue across ideological lines in order to break through the barriers that now prevent us from communicating with fellow human beings who live under social and political systems different from our own.

As for the People's Republic of China (PRC) and the conflict in Asia, statements of the declared policies of the PRC, the United States, and all other concerned parties should be carefully examined and evaluated against actual practice. Recognition of this divergence between declared and actual policies could lead to changes that might reduce enmity between the United States and China. The specific changes in policy recommended by the conference include several unilateral initiatives that need not require agreement from the Chinese or endanger legitimate interests of the United States or the security of those nations and peoples who rely on the United States.

In addition, the forms of intervention ought to be considered in terms of moral responsibilities and limitations. All acts of nations having effects on the internal affairs of other states must be scrutinized carefully against a background of moral and religious judgment. When particular acts involve military force with drastic consequences for the people of the affected nation, searching questions should be raised and answered concerning the possibility of substituting for unilateral intervention United Nations or other international action. Furthermore, the claims of human beings, whether allies, foes, or neutrals, as children of God must be a major factor in any moral assessment of available policy alternatives.

A Statement on Vietnam

We, the members of this National Inter-Religious Conference on Peace,

Ever mindful of the important formal statements on the war in Vietnam which have been made separately and recently by Pope Paul, by the Synagogue Council of America, by the National Council of Churches, by the World Council of Churches, and by other official groups,

Deeply concerned by the continuing and increasingly tragic consequences of that war,

Keenly sensitive to the moral issues involved in this entire sad situation, and especially in the consequential taking of many lives of innocent civilians,

Fully aware that the matter is complex and intense and solutions are not easy,

Do request and authorize the co-chairmen of this conference to ask a number of other major leaders of American religious bodies to join with them and together to seek a personal conference with the President at the White House for the purpose of respectfully urging upon the President that he:

1. Consider respectfully an immediate halt to the bombing in Vietnam,

2. Announce the readiness of the United States to join in a cease-fire of indefinite duration, beginning Good Friday, 1966, with no continuation of the build-up on either side,

3. Pursue every possible avenue, including channels of the United Nations, that may create more favorable circumstances under which negotiations can begin,

4. Adhere steadfastly to the principle that there cannot be a satisfactory military solution to this problem, and, until a negotiated settlement is achieved, not to permit a change in the character of the conflict through military escalation,

5. Agree to the direct representation of the National Liberation Front as well as the other concerned parties in any negotiations,

6. Maintain a determination to promote social and economic

change and progress in South Vietnam and to provide the people of that land an opportunity at an early date to choose their own government,

7. Continue providing reconstruction assistance and long-range economic development funds for Southeast Asia, and

8. Direct that high priority be placed in Vietnam upon patient, persistent peace-building programs, to overcome the dehumanizing and brutalizing effect, especially upon youth, of the twenty-year war.

We do further state expressly that we have confidence that this delegation of religious leaders will make their presentation to the President with a thoughtful and understanding knowledge of the conflicting advice and pressures to which he is ever subject and of the awesome responsibility and heavy burden which he now carries in the White House. For him and for all sharing his onerous responsibilities, we pledge our prayers.

We further suggest that most congressional leaders would welcome similar conversations and representations in which the delegates here bring to bear the thinking and moral guidance which legislators need in groping with the problems of maintaining the peace of the world.

A Proposal for Continuing Conferences

We ask the co-chairmen of this conference to continue the National Inter-Religious Conference on Peace Committee and to explore the possibilities for calling a World Inter-Religious Conference on Peace in 1967, encompassing participation of all the world's religious traditions.

We request the Synagogue Council of America, the National Council of Churches, the National Catholic Welfare Conference, and other religious bodies to join us in our call for a National Conference on Religion and Peace, along the lines of the earlier National Conference on Religion and Race.

We urge all religious, inter-religious, and community groups to intensify their work for peace. We recommend regional and local inter-religious conferences.

We commend the findings of this conference to the national religious organizations and to local membership of all religious bodies for study and—hopefully—guidance.

We urge all to pray with us for clarity of mind, integrity of spirit, and a deepening inter-religious fellowship that, under God, we may be guided through a night of our own making to a day when men shall know and love one another as God's children.

3

Conference Papers

A. LIVING WITH THE CHANGING COMMUNIST WORLD

This report was received by a plenary session of the conference. The first section was received for study by the plenary and commended for study and action. The recommendations were approved by participants in the plenary and addressed to organized religion everywhere, as well as to the general community and to the U.S. government.

The report is based on a position paper especially prepared for the conference by President Stewart Herman, Lutheran School of Theology, Rock Island, Ill.; Rabbi Robert J. Marx, Director, Chicago Federation of the Union of American Hebrew Congregations; Prof. Hans J. Morgenthau, Albert A. Michelson Distinguished Service Professor of Political Science and of Modern History, University of Chicago; Rev. John L. McKenzie, S. J., Divinity School, University of Chicago; and President Howard Schomer, The Chicago Theological Seminary, Chicago, Ill.

The workshop that discussed the position paper and transformed it into this report was chaired by Dr. E. Raymond Wilson, Secretary Emeritus, Friends Committee on National Legislation. The secretary was Rabbi Balfour Brickner, Director, Commission on Inter-Faith Activities, Union of American Hebrew Congrega-

tions. Discussants in this workshop at the conference were Prof. Buell Trowbridge, Department of International Affairs, American University; Mr. George T. Lister, Special Adviser, Office of Inter-American Security Affairs, U. S. Department of State; and the Rev. Werner-Christoph Schmauch, Methodist minister, New York City, and a member of the Committee of the Christian Peace Conference, Prague.

The drafting committee included Rabbi Balfour Brickner, Robert E. Jones, the Rev. Werner-Christoph Schmauch, President Howard Schomer, Hon. Harold E. Stassen (consultant), and Dr. E. Raymond Wilson.

1. The Evolution of Communist Societies in Theological Perspective

The Judaeo-Christian tradition understands the whole of human history as subject to the sovereign power of God. It sees historic events as happening in a universe that is meaningful, and human action as the crucial means by which the Ruler of history works out his moral purposes for life on earth, and perhaps also for the entire planetary system of which it is a part. The Judaeo-Christian tradition considers the effort to build a civilization and an international order that express God's creative purposes for life on earth to be the highest fulfillment of which man as earthling is capable. It presses toward a human society grounded in truth, built by justice, motivated by love, and realized in freedom. (See *Pacem in Terris,* par. 35.)

Because of this ultimate theological framework in which Jews and Christians seek to choose in each epoch among the various possible political options, they are aware that all political societies can and must evolve, and that all alike stand under Divine judgment. There they are disposed to appraise every political movement and social order primarily by its present fruits rather than by its original theoretical formulations, asking whether it is moving as best it can under existing circumstances toward growing justice and fraternity in freedom. Nowhere has this been better said than in the encyclical of Pope John XXIII, *Pacem in Terris*:

It must be borne in mind, furthermore, that neither can false philosophical teachings regarding the nature, origin and destiny of the universe and of man, be identified with historical movements that have economic, social, cultural or political ends, not even when these movements have originated from those teachings and have drawn and still draw inspiration therefrom. For these teachings, once they are drawn up and defined, remain always the same, while the movements, working on historical situations in constant evolution, cannot but be influenced by these latter and cannot avoid, therefore, being subject to changes even of a profound nature. Besides, who can deny that those movements, in so far as they conform to the dictates of right reason and are interpreters of the lawful aspirations of the human person, contain elements that are positive and deserving of approval? (par. 159)

Informed American Christians and Jews today tend to reject the doctrinaire and provincial approach that would condemn and combat every society stemming from other than Anglo-Saxon or other Western experience. While no such Jew or Christian would consider the ideology of either totalitarianism or *laissez-faire* an adequate formulation of the responsibilities of modern government, he would allow that, in particular situations, even inadequate forms of government may for a time be the only alternative to all-destructive civil or international violence.

The Sixth World Order Conference of the National Council of Churches of Christ on October 23, 1965, made specific application of this kind of theological understanding to the relationship of the United States with the several emerging Communist societies, and this paper endorses the wisdom of this Christian statement:

> Major changes have taken place in the Communist world . . . , and in our relations with it as Christians and Americans. . . . Christians can and should encourage every change in their own country or abroad which promises to render a given society, whether it knows it or not, more responsive to the rule of Christ. . . . Throughout the world the United States should be concerned to help nations to find alternatives to communism. But this means in practice that we should concentrate on helping nations to be themselves and to achieve viability and a capacity for independent life . . . we should not continue to con-

fuse the magnitude of our military power with its relevance. . . . The use of more and more force that destroys
more and more villages can be self-defeating as well as
cruel, for it weakens the stamina of the nation which we
seek to rescue from communism and it will have great
difficulty in preserving its independence. Our support
for democratic institutions and our anti-Communist convictions should not compromise our belief in the right of
a people to determine the form of government best suited
to its time and needs.

Communism No Longer Completely Monolithic

In a world currently undergoing profound social and political
internal change, it is necessary to recognize that the third of the
world's population which lives in Communist states is no longer
locked into a single, monocratic movement directed from one
power center in accordance with one over-all strategy toward one
global goal. The establishment of the People's Republic of China
in 1949, the death of Stalin in 1953, and the gradual relaxation of
Soviet Russian control in Eastern Europe since the 20th Party
Congress in 1956 have given rise to an increasingly polycentric
alliance of Communist governments that differ significantly in their
internal policies and in their responses to international events.

After forty years of unchallenged Russian domination of international communism, it is hard for many people and some governments to bring their set vision of the Communist world into line
with the emerging new reality. One of the acute sources of war
danger is the pursuit of policies by non-Communist governments
which presuppose a monolithic character and control in the Communist bloc. There are decision-makers and political groups in the
free world which have not yet begun to confront the changing
Communist scene in its full complexity, and so have an inadequate
grasp of the nature of the contemporary Communist challenge to
the political and economic hegemony of the West. In pastoral concern for the whole of humanity and for the growth of justice, reconciliation, and peace among all peoples, the responsible leaders
of the great religions of mankind need to help their diverse societies obtain a clearer view of each other and of the necessity of their
mutual accommodation for survival and for the resolution of their
urgent common problems.

It is over against this larger responsibility incumbent on all the world's religions that the particular peace tasks of religious bodies in the United States become evident. Together they number more than two thirds of the American nation, and that nation constitutes, by its economic, political, and military strength, the major power of the age: a fact that requires responsibility, not vaunting pride. Caught up in various phases of the ecumenical and interreligious movement, the churches and synagogues of the United States are in constant and meaningful communication with their counterparts in most of the nations of the world. Thanks to the basic freedom and independence of religion under the Constitution, they enjoy an unhampered access to the public mind in America. Nevertheless, there is a gap between pronouncements of church officials and organizational professionals and the practice of the layman. We are not unmindful of the responsibility of bringing these elements of life in closer rapport. This position paper therefore seeks to provide American religious persons, in their special quality as believers, with some guidelines for understanding the changes taking place throughout the Communist world, and seeks to suggest recommendations concerning the kind of American foreign policy toward Communist governments which is most likely to avoid escalating war and to aid the growth of peace, with justice and freedom. As we move toward coexistence and more effective co-operation across ideological lines, many American policies will have to change if we are to achieve success.

Communist Theories and Changing Societies

The recent changes in the Communist world—internal and international—correspond to the radical reinterpretation of Marxist doctrine. Since the beginning of the First World War, when the proletarians of all warring countries fought and killed each other instead of rising in unison against their capitalistic exploiters, historical experience has time and again demonstrated the fallaciousness of Communist analysis and prophecy. The denigration of Stalin at the 20th Party Congress in 1956 offers dramatic proof of this fact, as does the inadequacy of Marxism-Leninism in today's world. Thus Communists have increasingly turned to historic experience for guidance and are using Marxist-Leninist terminology to legitimatize their actions.

Internally, this ascendancy of experience over dogma has taken two main forms. Intellectual freedom appears to be growing, and a certain amount of criticism and a limited variety of differing opinions have been permitted. However, a society in which one group holds a virtual monopoly of political power, derived from an asserted monopoly of truth and virtue, can permit freedom of expression only within relatively narrow limits. Beyond these limits lies the self-destruction of the totalitarian monopoly through its dissolution into a plurality of philosophies and groupings of equal legitimacy.

Marxist dogma has a declining relevance in influencing action in the international sphere. Everywhere, and in different degrees, national feeling and the national interests of individual Communist governments and movements have begun to assert themselves. Thus the monolithic character of the world Communist movement, dominated by the Soviet Union, has been replaced by a variety of communisms, each pursuing its own national interests under the aegis of a common Communist philosophy. Roughly speaking, we can distinguish today at least four different types of communism: (1) subservient to the Soviet Union, such as that of Cuba, (2) subservient to China, such as that of Albania, (3) a generally independent national communism, such as that of Yugoslavia, and (4) a communism that vacillates between the Soviet Union and China and comes close to the Yugoslav type of communism, such as that of Rumania.

These different communisms compete with each other, as well as with the non-Communist world, and their relative positions are in dynamic flux. A communism at one time subservient to China may shift toward an independent or pro-Soviet position and vice-versa. American failure to understand these differences would stultify American foreign policy and prevent it from taking advantage of the new opportunities presented by the new dynamism of the Communist world.

II. *Evolution of U.S. Foreign Policy in Relation to the Communist World*

While in Eastern Europe the U.S. government distinguishes between different types of communism and adapts its foreign policy accordingly, in Asia, Africa, and Latin America it too often supports any kind of government that espouses anti-communism. Unfortunately, a large part of the American people are motivated by a fervid desire to stamp out communism everywhere.

A few of the principal phases of the U.S. government's response to the shifting challenge of Communist-led governments follow:

The first major American governmental reaction to the postwar moves of the Russian government, which included the imprisonment of the members of the Free Polish government upon their return from London, the sealing of the borders of the Eastern European states, and the open threats against Turkey and Greece, was the Truman Doctrine, formulated in 1947 and initiated with aid to Greece and Turkey.

The Truman Doctrine

The Truman Doctrine was based in part upon the concept that the issues between the United States and the Soviet Union should be understood, not as a rivalry between two great powers, but as a struggle between democracy and totalitarianism, between good and evil. It proclaimed the defense of free, democratic relations everywhere in the world against "direct or indirect aggression," against "subjugation by armed minorities or by outside pressure." It initiated the policy of containment of the Soviet Union. Thus, the Truman Doctrine transformed a concrete interest of the United States in a geographically defined part of the world into a moral principle of asserted world-wide validity, to be applied with an assertion that it was within the limits of American power and interests.

The Marshall Plan, motivated partly by anti-communism, had a far-reaching constructive effect on rebuilding postwar Europe. Unfortunately, the offer to include Russia and the Eastern European states was rejected by the Communist governments.

Dean Acheson, President Truman's Secretary of State, in his speech before the National Press Club on January 12, 1950, was thought by some to reduce the Truman Doctrine to the size of American national interest and to the power available to support it. It was the contrast between the sweeping generalities of the Truman Doctrine and the discriminating policies actually pursued by the Truman administration which was to become an issue in domestic politics for years to come. U.S. foreign policies, especially after the ascendency of the Chinese Communists on the mainland, were judged by the standards of the Truman Doctrine and were found wanting by the political opposition.

In 1950, firm military response to aggression in Korea gave a renewed meaning to the principle of the Truman Doctrine. It should be noted that this military action was under the U.N.'s auspices. The Korean aggression also led to further isolation and exclusion of the government of mainland China. Limited diplomatic contact in Warsaw has been followed only recently by the first slight relaxation by the United States of the ban on travel in China.

Under the stewardship of President Eisenhower and Secretary of State John Foster Dulles, the same emphasis on containment of communism was a major element of American policy, with added elements of massive nuclear deterrence and of openly expressed hope of eventual liberation of Eastern Europe. The Eisenhower administration formed anti-Communist alliances, such as the Baghdad Pact and SEATO, which were aimed to contain communism in the Middle East and Asia respectively.

President Eisenhower effected food distribution for the East Germans as well as for Yugoslavia and Poland. He also held the first postwar summit meeting in 1955, in which the ministers of the Soviet Union participated, as a result of which Russia and the United States enjoyed extensive cultural exchange. The Austria treaty was negotiated, and an openness was increasing until the U-2 incident.

Under President Kennedy the crusading spirit began to be replaced by recognition of the different types of communism and their impacts upon U.S. national interest. The nuclear test-ban treaty was a major milestone in Russian-American relations. This treaty was the only agreement reached in the years of persistent difficult negotiations for arms limitation and control and for disarmament.

Under President Johnson, pronouncements and policies vis-à-vis communism are, in one sense, more nearly aligned than in any earlier period. Anti-Communist doctrine appears to be in the process of becoming a program of global military action. The Secretaries of State and Defense have stated directly that we are fighting in Vietnam in order to stop Communist aggression throughout the world. The President himself has stated that "we do not propose to sit here in our rocking chair with our hands folded and let the Communists set up any government in the Western Hemisphere." In recent years, there has been an unprecedented direct use of American military combat force in unilateral action against communism.

Anti-Communism Not an Adequate Foreign Policy

Simple anti-communism is not an adequate basis for a sound American foreign policy. Revolutionary situations in large and different parts of the world necessitate different political responses.

In the first place, such a policy entails considerable risks; for the analysis may be mistaken or the policy may fail through miscalculation. Furthermore, and most importantly, such a policy is faced with a real dilemma. That dilemma is presented by the prospect of the rise of revolutionary movements in Asia, Africa, and Latin America, most, if not all, of which are likely to have a Communist component. In other words, any of these revolutionary movements may result in a Communist-type government.

In the face of this risk our government can choose between two different courses of action: (1) it can oppose all revolutionary movements around the world, in which case it would transform itself into the anti-revolutionary power, defending a *status quo* known to be unjust and in the long run indefensible; (2) it can make the rational choice, not between the *status quo* and revolution, but between non-Communist and different types of Communist revolutions. But it is our fear of communism that forces us into an anti-revolutionary stance *per se*.

On the other hand, if we refrain from intervening against those revolutionary movements, we risk their being taken over by their Communist component. It would then be left to our skill in political manipulation to prevent this Communist take-over from coming about, or, if it should come about, to prevent such a Communist revolution from becoming subservient to the Soviet Union or China. The United States would then have to compete with the Soviet Union and China in trying to influence these revolutions, taking the risk that not all those revolutions would remain under American sponsorship.

Such a policy would make the highest demands on the technical skill, the moral stamina, and the political wisdom of our government, but it is the only one that promises at least a measure of success. The alternative, the anti-Communist crusade, is in comparison simplicity itself. The domestic "consensus" supports it, and it makes but minimum demands on moral discrimination, intellectual subtlety, and political skill. The implementation is in essence a problem of military logistics: how to get the requisite number of armed men quickly to the theater of revolution. That task is easy, and we have shown ourselves adept at it. Yet the achievement of that task does not solve the problem of revolution. It smothers, as it were, the fire of revolution under a military blanket, but it does not extinguish it. And when that fire breaks out again with increased fury, the presuppositions of our policy have left us with no remedy but the commitment of more armed men trying to smother it again.

This policy is bound to be ineffective in the long run against the local revolution to which it is applied. It is also ineffective in its own terms of the anti-Communist crusade. For the very logic that makes us appear as the anti-revolutionary power *per se* surrenders to communism the sponsorship of revolution everywhere. Thus the anti-Communist crusade achieves what it aims to prevent: the exploitation of the revolutions of the age by the Soviet Union and China.

Finally, our reliance upon a simple anti-Communist stance and its corollary, military intervention, is bound to corrupt our judgment about the nature and the limits of our power. We flatter ourselves to defend right against wrong, to discharge the self-imposed duty to establish a new order throughout the world, and to do so effectively within the limits of military logistics. Thus we may well come to think that all the problems of the political world will yield to moral conviction and military efficiency, and that whatever we want to do we shall be able to do because we possess those two assets in abundance.

Recommendations

We are people whose focus extends beyond national interests and whose ultimate loyalties are greater than political partisanship. As members of various religious communities in the United States, many of us see in the changes of our world a continuing result of God's work in history. We are conscious that these changes may be a new manifestation of Divine judgment and providence to which we are challenged to respond in new ways.

1. We therefore encourage churches and synagogues in America to press for the kind of peaceful solutions of conflicts between the United States and Communist governments which will respect the legitimate political aspirations of all peoples and, in harmony with the basic Jewish and Christian ethos, will contribute to the growth of a co-operative world order. Emphasis should be placed upon the recognition of the diversity of Communist governments, and policy should be appropriate to each particular political, geographical, and military situation.

2. The central objectives of U.S. foreign policy toward the various Communist countries should be the development of normal diplomatic and cultural interchange, constructive response to internal liberalization, and the encouragement of their responsible participation in international organizations.

3. Many national societies are in need of drastic social change. The United States should make it clear in word and deed that it is the friend and supporter of needed change—even in face of the risk that revolutionary movements may come under Communist control. We reject the theory of many Americans that the United States must be the implacable foe of all forms of communism everywhere, as we reject the theory that we have an unqualified right to intervene militarily in any country where there is a danger of Communist revolution.

4. Wherever an indigenous revolutionary movement results in national Communist control, the United States should respond with dominant concern for the welfare of the local population and the interests of international peace.

5. As a nation that has benefited from constitutionality, federalism, and the rule of law, the United States has a responsibility to set an example of adherence to treaties, seeking always to refrain from unilateral action, in violation of existing international understandings, working instead through the U.N. and prepared to accept the judgment of properly constituted international agencies, including the U.N. and the World Court.

6. As concerned religious people, we believe that one of the ways in which our unique contribution can be best expressed is

through the initiation of personal contact, mutual religious inter-visitation, and the development of intensive dialogue across ideo-logical lines in order to break through the barriers that prevent us from perceiving as fellow human beings those whose social and political attitudes differ from our own.

We do not limit our contributions only to such contacts. We see as our mandate the expression, with increasing frequency, of our religious convictions in every possible form for America's on-going national debate on foreign policy. We must never hesitate to disagree vigorously with our government when it appears to vio-late religious ethics, or to support it when we believe its policies are sound and appropriate.

Our contribution should also be to encourage the use of non-violence in effecting needed social change. The effectiveness of non-violence has been demonstrated in the civil rights movement and in some movements toward independence. We believe that such action is a creative method for resolving conflict.

7. Economic imbalance between "have" and "have-not" na-tions is a major cause of political and social tension in our world. The advance of cybernation in the developed nations, the reality of hunger, want, and scarcity, intensify the disparity between the prosperous and the poor and pose a real and present danger to peace. We therefore call upon the Communist nations and the non-Communist nations, including the United States, to join in a massive co-operative effort to eradicate these evils from our world. Our mutual skills must be directed toward the technological de-velopment of agriculture and industry in the overpopulated and underfed nations. Moreover, we urge that economic aid be pro-vided on a massive scale, in different forms on a continuing multi-lateral basis.

8. Proper food is an elemental need of every human being; the right of access to it must never rest on the accident of birth or place of residence. We therefore encourage our government and the voluntary agencies in their efforts to lead the world in a war against hunger, and we urge that food and assistance in the neces-sary stimulation of food production be offered without regard to ideology.

9. We recommend support for universal membership in the U.N.

10. It is imperative that the world move toward the completion of a comprehensive test-ban treaty, a halt in the proliferation of nuclear weapons, and the making of rapid strides toward general disarmament in a system of world security based upon evolving world law and further development of international institutions. We urge all people to intensify their efforts for the achievement of these goals and we suggest that the American people in their search for security earnestly consider as well the security needs of our adversaries.

B. CHINA AND THE CONFLICTS IN ASIA

This report was received by a plenary session of the conference. The preamble and statement were received for study by the plenary and commended for study and action. The recommendations were approved by participants in the plenary and addressed to organized religion everywhere, as well as to the general community and to the U.S. government.

The report was based on a position paper especially prepared for the conference by Dr. Eugene Barnett, former General Secretary of the National Committee of the YMCA, Shanghai, 1922-36, and, upon his retirement in 1953, General Secretary of the National and International Committees, YMCA, New York City; Eugene Boardman, professor of history, University of Wisconsin, and during 1965-66 with the Friends Committee on National Legislation in Washington; and Father Joseph Sebes, S.J., associate professor of Far Eastern history, Georgetown University, Washington, D.C. Father Sebes also submitted a paper on "The State of Organized Religion in China Today."

The workshop that discussed the position paper and transformed it into this report was chaired by Rabbi Arthur Lelyveld, chairman, Committee on Justice and Peace of the Central Conference of American Rabbis and rabbi of Fairmont Temple in Cleveland. The secretary was Mr. James Finn, editor of World-view, a periodical of the Council on Religion and International Affairs. Discussants at the conference were the Rev. William Sloane Coffin, chaplain, Yale University and chairman of the National Emergency Committee of Clergy Concerned about Vietnam; Mr. Harold Jacobson, director of the Office of Asian Com-

munist Affairs, U.S. Department of State; and Prof. Stanley Millet, chairman, Department of Political Science, Adelphi University, Garden City, L.I.

Preamble

We approach the difficult problems of U.S.-Chinese relations as participants in an inter-religious conference sustained in our search for truth by the investigation of experts. Our concern is for the fulfillment of our shared ideals of justice and love, freedom and dignity.

It is of primary importance that we learn to see the 700 million people of the People's Republic of China first and foremost as fellow human beings, fellow inheritors of the splendors and travails of the earth, brothers because we are sons of the same God, who is Father over all. We believe that our failure to do so calls for repentance on our part, and a willingness to acknowledge our complicity in the enmity that presently characterizes U.S.-Chinese relations.

Peace is not merely the absence of war or the maintenance of some balance of power; it is "the fruit of love which goes beyond what justice can provide." This means that love, while it has nothing to do with appeasement, has everything to do with caring, and that there are no limits to the lengths to which a believer must go in order to achieve a world in which "each shall live under his own vine and under his own fig tree and none shall make them afraid." To work toward this kind of peace with the people of China must now become a major religious responsibility.

Statement

Since its establishment in 1949, the People's Republic of China (PRC) has striven to recover and reconstitute the traditional position of China in relation to areas of Asia on its borders. During the periods of its strongest dynasties, China controlled or required tribute from Korea and northern Indochina. Taiwan, until the Ming dynasty, was of little interest to mainland Chinese, and India, aside from the interest of Chinese Buddhists in the homeland of the Buddha, was remote. The Chinese Communists, jealous of China's place in the world, are now intent on making the fullest possible use of past precedent. China regards itself as a past victim of Western encroachment suffered under 100 years of the unequal treaty system (1842–1943) and therefore well equipped psychologically to help other countries recover from the encroachments of a colonial period. As one of the "have-not" nations with critical problems of population growth and agricultural production, China feels entitled to make common cause with other nations of Asia and Africa in a similar predicament. Finally, by virtue of their success in organizing China into a Communist state after thirty years of effort, the mainland Chinese aspire to the leadership of world communism and the spread of true Marxism-Leninism, criticizing Soviet leaders as revisionists and compromisers with capitalism and imperialism.

Employing one or more of these positions in varying degree, the Chinese Communists first co-operated with the U.S.S.R. over a wide field of endeavor, and then, following the withdrawal of Soviet advisers in 1960 and Soviet refusal to share atomic arms, sought to counter Soviet influence in Outer Mongolia and to stir up and exacerbate old border differences in Sinkiang and in the Amur region. Korea became the locus of Chinese involvement in 1950 when the approach of U.N. armies to the Yalu threatened South Manchurian industry and its sources of hydroelectric power. Chinese participation in the later phases of the Korean War and the truce negotiations resulted in China's replacing the Soviet Union as a main Communist support of North Korea. Though withdrawing its troops, Communist China continues to participate in the administration of the truce at Panmunjon and furnishes economic and political advice to the People's Republic of North Korea. Korean Communists defer to the Chinese today as did Korean Confucianists a century ago.

The PRC, unlike the listless Manchu dynasty, asserts its claim to Taiwan as an integral part of China, and makes the return of Taiwan a prerequisite to the settlement of all issues between itself and the United States. The Communist aim is to eliminate the Nationalist regime, which still insists it is planning the recapture of the mainland, using the offshore islands of Matsu and Quemoy as bases for intelligence and guerrilla provocation. The PRC asserts that it intends to end the American "imperialist" occupation and the rule of the reactionary clique of Chiang Kai-shek. At the moment, a Chinese Communist military move against Taiwan will provoke American retaliation as a military ally of the Nationalist Chinese.

China's interest in the war in Vietnam brings into play all the components of China's view of herself as a great power. The PRC tolerates no rival (such as the United States) so far as political leadership is concerned. South Vietnam is now the scene of a "war of national liberation" which, as a Communist nation, China is committed to support and to encourage. North Vietnam received Chinese aid and advice when it drove out the French twelve years ago. North Vietnam receives the same type of Chinese assistance in its support for the Vietcong in South Vietnam. The Chinese support refusal to negotiate in the hope of further engaging the Americans and lessening American power.

At the same time the PRC encourages rebellious Thai groups to weaken the Thai government and its American supporters. Until the recent attempted coup against the army in Indonesia, the Communist Chinese rejoiced in the growth of the Indonesian Communist Party and the growing alignment with President Sukarno.

In the other main area of Asian conflict, the Indian border, China's involvement has proceeded from reasons more connected with her pretensions to great power status than with the leadership of world communism. The Communization of Tibetan society, and the flight of the Dalai Lama and of thousands of Tibetan refugees to India, called for adjustment and better policing of the Indian border. Ambiguities in the MacMahon Line created claims and counter-claims and the makings of explosive conflict. Chinese desires to embarrass India, regarded as the exponent of a rival economic system, and to befriend Pakistan, regarded as a potential ally in the game of Asian power politics, are symptomatic of the moves of China as a great power. At the same time, Chinese cultivation of Nepal, Ceylon, Burma, and Cambodia reveal skillful practice of the arts of diplomacy.

Asian reactions to Chinese Communist activity have both a traditional and a modern aspect. Peripheral areas such as Korea and Indochina benefited in the past from a system of relations with China called the tribute system, which allowed the tributary nation a maximum of freedom from Chinese interference provided that diplomatic amenities were observed. Where the tributary relationship was not accompanied by conquest, as in the case of Korea, the feeling of the peripheral nation toward China was deferential and friendly. But where the peripheral nation experienced conquest and domination, as happened to northern Indochina, the result was to breed a deep resentment of the Chinese and a strong desire to be independent of Chinese direction. Indonesia and India, the other areas affected today, were too far from the center of traditional Chinese authority to be subject to either the tribute system or Chinese conquest. Taiwan, until the seventeenth century, was beneath imperial notice.

Since World War II, nations on China's periphery have manifested a flood tide of nationalism and revolution, largely a response to the colonialism and imperialism imposed on them for decades, and in some cases centuries. Colonial domination of Westerners over Asians, of white people over colored, of "Christians" over those of other religions, imposed a kind of unification and pacification, together with unnatural economic development through alien political and legal institutions, with the aim of financial profit and national prestige and power for the colonial ruler.

There were two logical outcomes of this alien barrage. The first was revolution, radical change in all spheres of society and culture, which has not yet reached its climax in Asia, Africa, and Latin America. The *status quo* of traditional society disappeared completely, being replaced either directly or indirectly by a new elite which arose under colonial rule. This new elite, new *status quo*, is going and should go, also, wherever it serves personal and small-group interests rather than the common good and national interests. The second offspring of colonialism was nationalism. Post-colonial nationalism, because it is a twin of revolution, demands not only political self-determination free of alien interference, but also, and of greater long-term significance, the creation of new patterns of society and culture adaptable to the technocracy of the West, but, at the same time, a manifestation of the distinctive national identity of these Asian societies and cultures. And in this great desire to enjoy the rich blessings of modern science and technology without becoming Western lies perhaps the greatest dilemma of Asian national revolutions. These revolutions, we must never forget, are different from the political revolutions of eighteenth- and nineteenth-century Europe and America and the nationalism of Western countries, because of their relation to imperialism and colonialism.

This is why America, despite its experience of a kind of nationalism and revolution, continues to underestimate, fails to comprehend, and insists on trying to play elder brother to them. The leaders in Peking ironically are experiencing the same difficulty, as is abundantly clear from recent events in Indonesia; Cuba and several African and Latin American nations are suspicious and fearful of both American and Chinese intervention in their revolutions, seeing in it a new threat of domination by alien interests. Many Asians feel that Peking works for their "liberation," i.e., bringing their revolution and nation under Communist-party control; that Washington supports "self-determination," i.e., the establishment of a government by military, urban elites whose political and economic orientation guarantees continued "co-operation" with American interests. Thus, both China and the United States are seen and felt to be offensive to their nationalism and subversive of their revolutions.

Understanding and accepting Asian nationalism and revolution in these terms is the first essential step toward a more realistic and effective policy that will lead toward reconciliation, the first concern of all religious people, and mature relationships with China and other Asian nations. But there is a second step no less essential for Americans. The unhappy and dangerous state of Sino-American relations, which has poised them as the giant adversaries in Asia, is as much due to actions based on America's ideology, mood, attitudes, and mystique as it is to China's. If there is to be any improvement in relations, America must change, as must China. What is required now is an honest, critical self-examination as to the reasons, motives, compulsions that fashion America's posture toward China and Vietnam. Dare we, can we, for example, expose the forces, the special groups and interests that have worked hard to fashion American ideology and stance, especially since 1945? Here is a clear possibility and imperative for action by religious groups in America.

The U.S. reaction to the current Chinese program is to view it as undisguised Communist aggression and to oppose it by force of arms in Vietnam and elsewhere by continuing a past effort to isolate and contain the Chinese. So the United States steadfastly denies to the PRC diplomatic recognition, trade, and all but minimal communication. The United States is an ally of the Republic of China on Taiwan, and for fifteen years has opposed entrance of

mainland China into the U.N. On their part, the Chinese Communists presently scorn the U.N. and behave as though they would
not accept membership if it were offered them. Meanwhile, settlement of the Vietnam situation and the necessity for talks on nuclear
disarmament call for Sino-American participation and co-operation. The achievement of a viable relationship with the PRC
looms as one of the most urgent problems for American foreign
policy and for the progress of peace. Consideration of this problem cannot be entertained without a statement on the war in
Vietnam.

The U.S. administration disavows the assumption that the current war in Vietnam is really a war against China, and yet, at other
times, declares that one purpose of our policy is to contain Communist China. We are deeply concerned with the failure of the
administration to initiate direct negotiations with all groups involved in the conflict and in particular with the National Liberation Front, which represents an important element of the population of South Vietnam.

It is clear that the situation in Vietnam has elements of both
civil war and revolution, but regardless of how we characterize
the war, the present tragedy is that the country is being steadily
defoliated and destroyed, and the lives of countless human beings
are being sacrificed. The continual escalation of the war and solutions sought solely through military means can have no result save
that of involving us eventually with China and hence in a total
war.

While we commend the administration for the efforts it has
already made to bring about negotiations, we appeal to our government to initiate an immediate cease-fire, to press for a negotiated
peace, and to co-operate in non-military plans for the rehabilita-
tion of Vietnam.

The U.S. government should immediately vastly increase its
economic aid in order to assist the Vietnamese people to rehabili-
tate their country. We have appropriated billions to achieve a dubious military victory. To alleviate the economic, social, and technological deficiencies, we have given only crumbs.

American Churches and China

American churches, through the missionary movement, have
in the past had many relationships with China and Chinese. A large

measure of responsibility for knowledge of and present attitudes toward China lies in the Christian missionary movement. Religious leaders thus have a responsibility in helping to bring about a better understanding of China today. In doing this, they are beset by the good and the bad in their history. Some American church leaders publicly deplored the effects of the unequal treaty system upon China and stated that they did not want to accept extraterritorial rights or the armed protection of U.S. gunboats patrolling China's inland waters. And yet they were part of a system that made China what Sun Yat Sen called a "half colony." All too few sought to share the living standards of their Chinese colleagues, and thus many came to be regarded as representative of a privileged group set apart. American missionaries, with their colleagues from other countries, were involved in helping to establish institutions of higher education in China, to provide education for women, to establish medical standards, to develop modern journalism, to provide relief in times of famine and disaster. The Christian faith was one of the factors involved in the modernization of Chinese society. Some American church leaders aligned themselves with the Nationalist government; this plus the fact that they were inevitably aligned with U.S. policy meant that they suffered repudiation when the Chinese Communists came to power. This had deep effects on Chinese Christians who have had in the new era to make clear their identification with China. Although cut off from all direct contact with Chinese churches, American church leaders have continued their interest in China and the Chinese, hoping and praying for the time when the Chinese churches would once again take their rightful place in a world-wide Christian fellowship on a basis of mutuality and respect.

America should realize with humility that Chinese intransigence stems in part, not only from 100 years of Chinese subservience under the unequal treaty system, but also from such memories as these:

In the 1920's Americans helped Sun Yat Sen in his social reforms so little that he had to turn to the Russians for help. In the 1930's when Japan attacked, Chinese were being killed by Japanese bombs made of American scrap metal. In the 1940's, by intervention in China's internal affairs, America helped prolong a civil conflict, thereby adding to Chinese suffering and resentment. In 1956 China proposed an exchange of newsmen; in 1958 a "nuclear-free" Pacific; and after the explosion of its own bomb, China invited all nuclear powers to conference. America missed all three opportunities by refusing even to enter into negotiations. Finally, the United States has consistently refused to recognize the People's Republic of China and steadfastly opposed its seating in the U.N.

Religious organizations today are bound to try to seek ways of understanding and reconciliation with China. They are bound to try to solve conflicts of interest and purpose within the framework of existing institutions and peaceful procedures. They should devote themselves to the re-establishment of contact and improvement of communication. They should lead in efforts to discover and understand the causes of hostile attitudes. Further, it must be realized that by and large the Asian world is a food-deficient area. It behooves wealthy nations such as the United States to try by measures of aid, direct supply, and advice to remove all causes of aggression that grow from food shortages. Western religious leaders should realize with humility, too, that part of Chinese intransigence stems from 100 years of Chinese subservience under the unequal treaty system.

We are conscious of the fact that the PRC has restricted the activities of Chinese religious believers to little more than worship. The activities of education, social service, and medicine formerly performed by religious bodies are now the sole province of the state. Also, Chinese religious believers are required to demonstrate their allegiance to the domestic and international policies and programs of the nation and are organized with special patriotic groups for this purpose. All foreign financial support, advice, and direction has been discontinued. Chinese religious bodies are now on their own in a period of trial, and face an uncertain future.

As religious believers we are keenly interested in sharing the quest for religious truth with the people of China, seeking no longer to direct missions but to communicate with co-religionists on a basis of equality and shared interest. The achievement of such communication is a fundamental component of the improved relationship we seek with China.

Recommendations

In a thermonuclear age, where international conflicts portend the total destruction of mankind, both the moral imperatives and the practical concerns of national security require the lessening of international tensions. This would be in the best national interest, not only of the United States and China, but of all men everywhere. In order to improve the relationship between the United States and the People's Republic of China, American leaders should strive to initiate positive programs designed to solve our differences through peaceful methods. Measures to be taken should include the following:

1. Promote actively a program of communication, intervisitation, and exchange with the people of the PRC. Sino-American misunderstanding is compounded by the almost complete absence of communication between our people. The result is American public ignorance of China and Chinese ignorance of us, a dangerous condition that builds up tensions. While the U.S. government does not now oppose the interchange of physicians, journalists, and scientists, it should approve the invitations to Chinese counterparts of American visitors, actively encourage every form of communication, and repeal legislation forbidding the entrance of Communist individuals to this country. We hope that the Chinese will understand that such communication and interchange is to our mutual advantage.

2. End all special restrictions on trade in non-strategic items. Such trade could be opened unilaterally and quickly as a simple administrative decision. It would offer concrete evidence of a change in attitude toward China.

3. Support negotiations for Sino-American co-operation in the fields of medicine, population control, soil fertilization, and plant genetics, so that China's goal of a viable economy can be furthered. The exchange of knowledge in these fields could improve relations between our two peoples.

4. Co-operate in measures for nuclear and conventional disarmament. Need exists all along the line for Sino-American communication in the field of arms control. Efforts should continue to invite China to a world-disarmament conference and as a member of the Eighteen-Nation Disarmament Committee.

5. Move toward settlement of the international position of Taiwan, mindful of the wishes of the Taiwanese. Talks should be initiated through the services of an international negotiating body under U.N. auspices and to include all concerned parties. They would have to proceed from a recognition of the fact that the PRC is the government of China and the Republic of China is actually the government of Taiwan.

6. Urge the withdrawal of the Republic of China's forces from the offshore islands of Quemoy and Matsu. The removal of this tense confrontation would hopefully lead to negotiations and the substitution of peaceful methods for the present threat and counter-threat. Provision would have to be made for the safety, security, and rights of the present civilian residents.

7. Support the seating of the PRC in the U.N. on the basis of the principle of universality of membership in the U.N. of all sovereign states. China's participation in the Specialized Agencies and in the many working subcommittees and political caucuses would provide international participation by China as a member of the community of nations.

C. INTERVENTION: MORALITY AND LIMITS

The report below was received by a plenary session of the conference. Unlike the reports of the other two workshops, this was not as easily divided into 1) preliminary material received for study by the plenary and commended for study and action and 2) recommendations approved by participants in the plenary and addressed to organized religion everywhere as well as to the general community and the U.S. government.

This report grew out of a position paper especially prepared for the conference by Dr. Jacob B. Agus, rabbi and author; Mr. Tilford Dudley, member Program Board, Division of Christian Life and Mission, National Council of Churches; and Dr. Arthur I. Waskow, resident fellow, Institute of Policy Studies, Washington, D.C., and author.

The workshop which discussed the position paper and transformed it greatly (see Appendix of this volume) was chaired by Msgr. Edward G. Murray, secretary-treasurer of the conference and pastor of Sacred Heart Church, Roslindale, Mass. The secretary was Mr. Herman Will, Jr., Division of Peace and World Order, General Board of Christian Social Concerns of The Methodist Church. Discussants at the conference were Dr. William E. Moran, Jr., dean, School of Foreign Service, Georgetown University, Washington, D.C.; Harold E. Stassen, Esq., member, Philadelphia Bar, former Special Assistant to the President and U.S. Represen-

tative to the Disarmament Subcommittee, and past president of the American Baptist Convention; and Dr. Gordon Zahn, professor of sociology, Loyola University, Chicago, Ill., and author of In Solitary Witness.

The drafting committee included the Rev. Sidney Lovett of the Rock Spring Congregational Church in Arlington, Va., in addition to Rabbi Agus, Dean Moran, Msgr. Murray, and Mr. Will.

Religion stimulates us to a moral appraisal of intervention and the circumstances giving rise thereto for three specific reasons:

a) By faith we believe that the ultimate claim and sovereignty of God stands above any other claim or loyalty.

b) We believe God calls us to righteous obedience in loving service to our fellow men.

c) Furthermore, to be consonant with God's call, any means must be consistent with the ends sought.

Religious men, therefore, are compelled to exercise moral sensitivity within the structures of their social life. Our common ethical imperative is to love one another. An individual may exercise this imperative more radically (even sacrificially) than corporate bodies, which, of necessity, seek a tolerable blending of diverse interests and the need for order. Corporate structures (the state, trade associations, unions, even religious organizations) are not thereby immune from moral judgment of their behavior. Groups are morally obligated to seek higher forms of effective love. In the corporate affairs of men, justice is love's tutor, not master. It recognizes the necessity of power to restrain the unjust; it counsels the powerful with restraint. Justice alone is not enough. It must be tempered by love.

In the past, religious people have lacked clarity of purpose and tenacity of will in the search for peace, well-being, and dignity. Too often we have failed in time to awaken the people to the moral responsibilities which the search for peace places upon us. The times demand new awareness and new commitment to peace.

Intervention, defined in the broadest terms, includes any action by a nation which affects significantly the social, economic, or political life of another nation. In the twentieth century, mankind has defined its political life along national lines. Only in limited circumstances has national sovereignty been effectively shared with international organizations. The heightened spirit of nationalism has been accompanied by the technical revolution, which has created such interdependence among nations that intervention is inevitable. This is not simply a matter of the strong affecting the weak, for the weak also can and do affect the strong. Intervention takes many forms: armed force, trade, cultural exchange, propaganda, technical assistance, etc. Even as there are many forms, there are various reactions to intervention. One form may contain threats to a government's survival, whereas another may hold promise for a better life, and the nations involved may achieve a tolerable guest-host relationship. Intervention should point toward transforming justice and the increase of fair opportunity for all the people of the country affected.

We warn against the temptation to national idolatry whereby nations assume that they possess transcendent power or virtue. There should be moral responsibilities and moral limits to all forms of intervention. In particular, the bombing of centers of civilian population, whether by nuclear or conventional means, and the murder or torture of prisoners of war can never, under any circumstances, be justified. It is the obligation of every government to oppose and prevent such acts, whether by its own forces or by those associated with it in arms. Under God, every human being has an innate dignity that must be respected.

All peoples have the right to develop and determine their own pattern of life and government. Even in the event of major rebellion, there should be no unilateral coercive intervention. All efforts should be made to achieve peace and order through appropriate international bodies. Were there international agreement to prevent the supplying of arms to the developing countries beyond those necessary for essential national police efforts, the extent of social upheaval which must be anticipated in those countries would be greatly reduced.

The present limited capacity of the United Nations to deal effectively with some of the most divisive and dangerous instances of intervention highlights the need for substantial progress in international organization. Current threats to peace require that the U.N. be given the authority, the funds, and the means with which to act promptly and forestall unilateral action by national states. To accomplish such a change, the peoples of the member states of the U.N. must be mobilized in support of such actions and their governments brought to accept appropriate national policies. However, until substantial progress is made in the reduction of national armed forces under a universal system of disarmament, with effective inspection and control, the possibility will remain that great power action may thwart the success of international peacekeeping operations.

> Today the universal common good poses problems of world-wide dimensions which cannot be adequately tackled or solved except by the efforts of public authority endowed with a wideness of powers, structure and means of the same proportions: that is, of public authority which is in a position to operate in an effective manner on a world-wide basis. The moral order itself, therefore, demands that such a form of public authority be established. (*Pacem in Terris,* Par. 137)

We urge the co-chairmen of the National Inter-Religious Conference on Peace to call at once upon the leaders of world religious bodies to convene a World Inter-Religious Conference on Peace. We would hope that such a conference might lead to the formation of a Permanent World Forum to study and review those situations where armed conflict exists or is probable and to make recommendations as to how such conflict may, with justice, be ended or avoided.

Vietnam

South Vietnam offers an example of just such a conflict. The United States is present with military force in large number, stating that these forces are in Vietnam in fulfillment of treaty obligations, to contain communism, and to provide the South Vietnamese with an opportunity for free elections.

Our insights as religious people do not allow us to support an all-out war for the above purposes. The American people, in general, have given support to their government, but with an uneasiness unknown in almost any previous war experience. There is no easy moral way out of the present predicament; but we are certain that there is no way to justify morally an indefinite continuance of the war in all its inhumanity. We note the difficulty that each side has in accepting a peace conference with an opponent who sets

forth terms that seem tantamount to surrender. Yet the war bears
heavily upon both sides, and procedural difficulties which one day
will have to be faced should be faced and settled now.

The danger of new pressures for escalation of the war resulting from impatience and disappointment is grave. Such an escalation would not only fail to achieve the declared goals of the United
States; it might ultimately involve the world in a war of mutual
destruction.

We therefore respectfully urge the Administration to:

1. Consider an immediate halt to the bombing in Vietnam;

2. Announce the readiness of the United States to join in a
cease-fire of indefinite duration, beginning Good Friday, 1966,
with no continuation of the build-up on either side;

3. Pursue every possible avenue, including channels of the
U.N., that may create more favorable circumstances in which
negotiations can begin;

4. Adhere steadfastly to the principle that there cannot be a
satisfactory military solution to this problem, and until a negotiated settlement is achieved, not to permit a change in the character
of the conflict through military escalation;

5. Agree to the direct representation of the National Liberation Front as well as the other concerned parties in any negotiations;

6. Maintain its determination to promote social and economic
change and progress in South Vietnam and to provide the people
of that land an opportunity at an early date to choose their own
government; and

7. Continue providing reconstruction assistance and long-
range economic development funds for Southeast Asia.

Addendum

In a sense, simply to be is to intervene, for does not each of us
in some measure enter the life of every other? Recognizing, then,
that intervention begins with individual existence as such, we urge
upon each individual the prior moral assessment of possible actions involving him either as person or as citizen. We would
specifically assent to the following paragraph:

Since the right to command is required by the moral order and has its source in God, it follows that, if civil authorities pass laws or command anything opposed to the moral order and consequently contrary to the will of God, neither the laws made nor the authorizations granted can be binding on the consciences of the citizens, since "God has more right to be obeyed than men." (*Pacem in Terris,* Sec. 51)

In this respect, attention is called to the specific teachings of our various religious traditions concerning permissible and impermissible uses of violence, the just-war doctrine, etc., for by their light each specific conflict ought to be judged, and individual participation determined.

That this exercise of individual conscience be fully respected, it is incumbent upon governments to recognize the right of conscientious objection, not only to all wars as such, but also to specific conflicts where, in the judgment of the individual, basic moral teachings are being violated.

4

The Issue of Peace: The Voice of Religion

Dr. John C. Bennett

A statement on religion and peace should begin with some affirmations about the bases that our churches and synagogues have for speaking and acting in the sphere of international relations.

Underlying all else that we may say or do here is the biblical faith that God is Lord of our nation and of all nations. As the prophet said: "All the nations are as nothing before him, they are accounted by him as less than nothing and emptiness" (Is. 40:17). As Amos said earlier: "Did I not bring up Israel from the land of Egypt, and the Philistines from Caphtor and the Syrians from Kir?" (9:7). The faith that all nations are under the judgment and providence and mercy of God is central to biblical religion. As it is the nation that so easily becomes the ultimate object of loyalty for its citizens, this faith in God transcending the nation is always a warning against national idolatry. And in our time it is political idolatry, the worship of any social group or system, that is the greatest obstacle to the tolerance and humaneness which are essential conditions for decent relations among nations, essential conditions for peace. The form that idolatry takes with people of some sophistication is not so much the explicit worship of the nation as it is the assumption that God is always on the side of one's own nation, an easy assumption when our adversaries are atheists!

A second basis for all that we say or do may be ultimately derived from Biblical faith, but even without being aware of its religious background many people are, fortunately, able to see the truth of it and to be claimed by it for their own lives. I refer to the moral imperatives that, when translated into a social ethic that is relevant to public life, call us to care for the welfare and dignity of all neighbors including enemies, to seek for them justice and freedom. When I speak of justice, I mean a transforming justice that continually raises the level of life of those who have been at a disadvantage. Most of our neighbors in the world are victims of poverty and hunger. Only a revolutionary justice can help them. This is not to suggest that there are some religious shortcuts to the proper balance in our world of justice and freedom, both of which depend upon some kind of political order. But our religious imperatives do press upon us to seek these values. Our churches and synagogues should continually disturb us and press us to do what is in our power to deliver God's people everywhere from poverty and hunger, from humiliation and oppression, from anarchy and war.

Our problems begin when at a given time we find the quest of one value such as freedom interfering with another such as order or justice. There will be some differences of opinion about this, but I believe that a conference on peace should begin by recognizing that peace is not the only good, that at times it may have to be sacrificed for the sake of other goods. And yet we may still say that total war would probably destroy all the goods for which we strive and that the burden of proof upon those who defend even limited wars must be a heavy one, for limited wars may escalate into total war, and nations, including our own, have a habit of assuming too uncritically the moral and political efficacy of military solutions.

I shall add to these bases for what we may do here one more: a realistic understanding of the temptations to which nations are especially vulnerable. Reinhold Niebuhr has a chapter in his *Moral Man and Immoral Society* on the "morality of nations." This is a classic statement of the situation. Let me mention two of his chief emphases: The first is that "patriotism transmutes individual selfishness into national egoism." This enables good men to become the instruments of the pride and ambition and greed of nations. He also emphasizes the tendency of nations, including the United States, to clothe the national will with idealistic pretensions. He says that "perhaps the most significant moral characteristic of a nation is hypocrisy." This is a hard saying, but I recommend this chapter as devotional reading to all the speech writers in Washington or in any capital.

Professor Herbert Butterfield emphasizes the way in which democracies especially become victims of their own frenzied national self-righteousness. He makes much of the idea that the most furious and cruel conflicts are between what he calls "giant organized systems of self-righteousness," with each system only too delighted to find that the other is wicked, each only too glad that the sins give it the pretext for still deeper hatred and animosity (*Christianity, Diplomacy and War*). This is a fairly accurate description of the relations between the United States and China.

George Kennan reminds us of our own national frenzy in the first world war when our enemy was the Germany of Kaiser Wilhelm II, a moderate compared with subsequent adversaries. Kennan says: "There is, let me assure you, nothing more egocentrical than the embattled democracy. It soon becomes the victim of its own propaganda. It then tends to add to its own cause an absolute value which distorts its own vision of everything else. *Its* enemy becomes the embodiment of all evil, *its* own side, on the other hand, is the center of all virtue" (*Russia and the West Under Lenin and Stalin*).

National self-examination and national repentance are difficult though not impossible. But citizens, each with his own background of faith and commitment, can and do repent on behalf of their nations. A national repentance usually depends upon events, often catastrophic events, which convince men of ordinary prudence that the nation has been following a wrong road. One of the responsibilities of churches and synagogues is to interpret such events.

Let me at once put in a corrective for what I have said: from such a statement about the temptations of nations it would be a great error to deduce that we should therefore say "a plague on all houses" and hold ourselves aloof in personal self-righteousness from all of the strivings of our government. We may be tempted to become personally self-righteous because of our criticism of national self-righteousness. Nations at the present time are the only units of power that can do many things that need to be done. Nations have responsibilities that are commensurate with their power. National ideals are not necessarily mere rationalizations of crude national interests. Also, what is in the real national interest of the citizens of a nation has its proper claim so long as it is not dressed up with idealism and ideology and made into an absolute.

Whatever the errors and self-deceptions of the United States, our country was not wrong about the threat of Hitlerism to humanity and it was not wrong about the need to develop power in the defense of Western Europe against Stalinism. The United States is right today in trying to keep as much of the world as possible open so that nations may choose their own social systems; but it does exaggerate the role of military force in this effort, it is guided by a persistent notion of American omnipotence, and it does clothe its policies with far too simple ideas of freedom and with too absolutistic an anti-communism.

I come now to a question that is asked on all sides whenever churches and synagogues or their leaders speak about these problems of foreign policy and international relations. It has been said that these high matters belong to the experts or to policy-makers on the spot who live with the changing details of the problems and who may have access to classified information. We are often believed to be outsiders who are said to have no competence to speak.

It is very difficult to disentangle the moral factors from the technical and in the broadest sense strategic factors in any complicated situation. Nevertheless, there are at least six areas in which persons who combine religious perspectives and moral sensitivity with a careful attempt to understand the relevant facts, though not specialists or insiders in the government, have a duty and right to speak.

First, they have a duty and a right to call attention to the immediate human consequences of any policy. This in itself may not be decisive, because there is always the question of the probable human consequences of changing the policy. Yet, this question should not silence the critic. The human consequences of an alternative policy in many cases may be quite speculative, and however one judges that, what our nation may now be doing to people needs to be kept to the fore.

Second, the determination of the goals of policy is a matter of moral choice. Dean Acheson, in his provocative speech at Amherst College in 1964 about morality and foreign policy, was right in dismissing many moral slogans as inadequate guides to policy; but, when he came to his own statement of the goal of American policy, he said that our goal was "to preserve and foster an environment in which free societies may exist and flourish." Is not his own phrase "free societies" another one-sided moral slogan? How is this freedom to be related to a transforming justice and to order and viability in a nation in a period of tumultuous and revolutionary change?

Without taking time for analysis, I shall dogmatically state four goals that should guide our policy. They are all moral goals, but they are all consistent with a wise estimate of the conditions for our own national welfare and security in the long run. They are as follows: (1) the prevention of war and especially the prevention of the escalation of any conflict into general nuclear war; (2) the preservation of as wide an area as possible of openness in the world in which nations have freedom to choose their own social systems, in which there is diversity and mutual respect among those who choose diverse paths; (3) the helping of nations that are struggling against hunger and poverty to achieve justice and access to plenty and to do so in their way and not necessarily in our way; (4) support for the United States and development of its functions to enable nations to find security and multilateral substitutes for the present arms race, to extend the rule of law among nations and encourage the growth of mutual confidence and human relations between them. At any given moment there may be a fierce debate among moralists concerning the priority that is to be assigned to each of these goals. This is where morality necessarily becomes contextual. But let no context in which we may be called to act obscure any one of them. The assignment of priorities is not a matter for the expert alone. It does not depend on classified information. It should not be the monopoly of the policy-maker. It should be a subject of continuous national discussion to which churches and synagogues can make an essential contribution.

The *third* area of moral concern has to do with the means used to achieve any or all of these ends. Here there will be much debate among us between those who represent a religious pacifism and those who believe that we must allow for the use of military force to check force or to overcome oppression. I belong to the latter group, but the issues are so difficult that I often wish that I did not. For one thing, I am much impressed today by the probability that even uses of force which have some justification easily escalate and, even when this process remains limited, do more harm than good. Can we not agree on two forms of limitation of force? One is that we should not use bombs, nuclear or conventional, against centers of population as was done in the second world war and as our own government now threatens as a last resort. I know that we are at a stage in which it is plausible to allow some license to what may be called "deterrent talk" even though it is murderous. I am not clear about this myself except that I believe that this cannot go on for long without being very much a source of moral corruption to a nation that engages in it. The other form of limitation of force is to resolve never to use nuclear weapons first. There are difficult technical problems here mixed with moral problems; for example, problems involving the differences between types of nuclear weapons and their relation to conventional weapons.

While we discuss these matters in general terms, we should give strong support to those in our government who resolutely refuse to bomb Hanoi or to extend our bombing to China. If it is true that the President feels stronger pressure from those who would expand the war than he does from those who would restrict it or end it now, whatever else we may think about our policy in Vietnam, we should be able to agree on our responsibility to counteract that pressure.

A *fourth* area in which religious groups can make a contribution is in helping the American people to see the world as it appears to other countries and especially as it appears to people in Asia, Africa, and Latin America—for they get less of a hearing among us than the European nations. Our churches have close relations with the churches in these other continents. What we hear from our fellow churchmen there reflects much more than an inside church point of view; it reflects widely held views in their nations.

Let me give one illustration of this kind of contribution: the General Board of the National Council of Churches, in a message to the American churches last December, put great emphasis on the self-defeating character of our action in Vietnam because of its effects on the sensibilities of Asians. Here is one very forthright statement:

> We believe that if the United States follows a unilateral policy in Vietnam, no conceivable victory there can compensate for the distrust and hatred of the United States that is being generated each day throughout the world because we are seen as a predominantly white nation using our overwhelming military strength to kill more and more Asians.

The Central Committee of the World Council of Churches made a similar statement in February:

> The primary objective must be to stop the fighting as the most effective step to starting discussions and negotiations. This is not an easy task and we are not unaware of the deep-rooted obstacles which have thus far prevented progress from the battlefield to the conference table. This is all the more urgent because by continuing the conflict both sides face acute problems. On the one hand the United States of America and its allies face increase of bitter racial and other resentments against the West, and on the other hand the Vietnamese face the vast destruction of their people and resources. The prospect of victory at the end of the conflict does not justify this inevitable cost.

I do not suggest that churches have a monopoly of wisdom concerning the more intangible effects of our policies on other peoples, but they do have an inside track to this kind of understanding, and it is easy for the policy-makers and experts in any one country to be so absorbed with a problem from the dominant point of view in their country that they fail to see how self-defeating their policies may be. Also they often gain a vested interest in policies and so, rather than admit an error, they extend the range of their commitment in the hope of proving that they were right. This need not be a conscious process.

The *fifth* area in which those who are not specialists and those who are not policy-makers on the spot may make a contribution has to do with the presuppositions of policy, expressed or unexpressed. Is it not probable that on important matters of foreign policy which go beyond limited tactical decisions, our makers and defenders of policy are governed less by facts of which they may have a monopoly than they are by various assumptions about our period of history? Assumptions on many matters are determinitive, e.g., about the dynamics of communism in its various stages, about the role of military power in the containment of communism in a revolutionary situation, about the meaning of social revolution on other continents, about the place of freedom in relation to other values, about the relevance of our experience in dealing with Hitler and Stalin in Europe to the way in which we deal with problems in Asia, about the degree of the risks of nuclear war involved in our policy and about our moral right to take such risks. Military expertise is no guarantee of wisdom about any one of them. And on some of them decisions may be made on the highest level on the basis of an unexamined line of thought that has become dominant.

Churches and synagogues have no monopoly of wisdom about these matters either, but they do have their contribution to make. These issues belong to the sphere of public debate. They need the widest possible ventilation from all sides with many voices heard from other countries. I believe that at the present time, especially in relation to Asia and Latin America, our policy-makers are in a rut about many of these issues.

A *final* contribution the churches and synagogues can make to the national discussion of these issues is to criticize the false uses of religion and morality which are so common. This means criticism of the psychology of the "holy war" that is one factor in the American attitude toward the cold war. This means alertness concerning all forms of national self-righteousness. It also calls for a continuous examination of the use of such words as "honor," "obligation," and "commitment," when our policy in Vietnam is defended by spokesmen in government. "Honor" is an especially ambiguous word, and it is difficult to distinguish between its use to refer to national face-saving and its use to refer to a genuine moral obligation.

I shall limit myself to a discussion of one of these issues which seems to be most pervasive, and that is the view we hold of communism. At the present time in many situations one major source of error in the determination of policy is an absolutistic anti-communism. I do not believe that this is always so, for in relation to European communism this outlook has been in large measure abandoned. The breaking of the Communist monolith by the Sino-Soviet split, the gradual humanization of society in the Soviet Union and most of the Eastern Communist countries, the diverse paths taken by these Eastern European nations—these developments fortunately have influenced American policy. We now know intellectually, even if this knowledge is not fully absorbed, that for a nation to become Communist does not mean that it is lost for all time to Stalinist slavery. The American rhetoric of a decade ago that kept contrasting the "free world" with the "slave world" has fortunately disappeared in the highest circles of government, though to a considerable extent it continues to influence the public.

No influence has been more helpful in counteracting the American anti-Communist obsession than that of Pope John XXIII and the Vatican Council. Pope John did much to expel the holy-war psychology in relation to communism from his church and from other churches. It is most significant that the Vatican Council refused to take action condemning communism and that it initiated steps leading to dialogue with atheists, including Marxist atheists.

Yet the American obsession with anti-communism keeps appearing, especially when we seem ready to declare that we must oppose all wars of liberation in Asia and Latin America if they are inspired by one of the branches of international communism.

I believe that we should help nations that can be helped to find alternatives to communism because, however much a Communist society may improve after some decades, it does bring terror and tyranny in the early stages to any country that embraces it. I do think that we should put over against this fact the recognition that Communists have no monopoly on terror. The recent slaughter of Communists in Indonesia by the hundreds of thousands should remind us of this. Political cruelty on all sides in tumultuous situations is so common that it should gain our attention more than it does.

The axiom that communism is the worst fate that can ever come to any country is false. It may not be worse than years and years of civil war; it may not be worse than some rightist tyrannies; it may not be worse than some decades or even generations of neglected social and economic problems. Communism is cruel in its early stages and it has not been successful in dealing with all problems, the problem of agriculture, for example. But after the revolutionary period it does become in many ways constructive; it does overcome anarchy, it does deal radically with famine and poverty and disease and illiteracy. If it can be gradually human- ized, as it is in European Communist countries, our nation should not take all measures to prevent a nation in Asia from becoming Communist. It may be that people will vote themselves into com- munism, but how far self-determination in this sense can be a reality in situations of civil war and revolution is debatable. One fine day there might be a free election, but what is to prevent its results from being overturned six months later? The pressure and counter-pressure of political movements in such situations seem to determine the fate of nations whether there are elections or not. We in America do not like to have it so, but there are some things that are beyond our control, and when we try to control them we may do far more harm than good, despite fine motives.

I cannot speak of communism without dealing with China. As we face the reality of China as a vast human power—whether it is moved primarily by communism or by nationalism—churches and synagogues have no expert knowledge of what is happening in that country; nor can they read the minds of the Chinese leaders, those who will pass from the scene or those soon to assume power. The doctrines and slogans of the Chinese which seem to scare our De- fense Department are paranoiac, even though Chinese behavior has so far been prudent and cautious. Who is to decide how signif- icant the doctrines and the slogans are? James Reston raises the question as to whether this is for the Defense Department to de- cide. Without attempting to decide, we can ask ourselves some questions.

Communism has been the instrument by which China has been unified, by which it has become able to assert itself among the nations, by which it has been able to purge itself of the effects of generations of humiliation at the hands of the white West. Why must we take all that China does now against us with such serious- ness and forget for how long she has been the victim of the Western powers of which this nation is now chief representative? Why must we have a double standard and do near the borders of China

what we would never allow China to do near our borders? Why
are we still involved in the Chinese civil war as the major ally of
Nationalist China? Is there no possibility of our changing our attitudes toward China even though we know that a tragic history
and the fanaticism of early communism make it unlikely that China
will soon change her attitude toward us? How long are we to be
engaged in diplomatic efforts to keep Communist China isolated?
Should our policy not be designed with all the imagination we can
muster to undercut the paranoia of China, not exacerbate it?

In our religious communities there should be continued efforts
to counteract national attitudes in regard to China. The General
Board of the National Council of Churches called recently for a
reversal of American policies that are designed to isolate China
and for preparation for the widest variety of relations between the
United States and China.

China today is relatively weak. If we take advantage of her
weakness to keep her down, to deny her even her natural role as
the greatest power in Asia, a role that we assume for ourselves in
this hemisphere, if we isolate her and continue to express our own
hostility against her, punctuated by moral lectures, we may find
ourselves face to face fifteen years from now with a powerful China
that has every reason to seek revenge upon us. I do not say that
this prospect should be the main motive for a change of attitude
and a change of policy, but it does indicate the kind of judgment
that will come upon us if we do not do so.

Churches and synagogues should provide an environment in
our country within which these questions are continually raised
and in which new attitudes can begin to form. I hope and pray
that new relationships will become possible between our religious
communities and the people of mainland China. We often hear
that our government would like to change its policy in many re-
spects but that it is afraid of the people. If so, let us do what we
can to support its desire for change among the people and let us
ask the representatives of government to give some leadership if
they do seek such change.

One final word. I have said very little about the U.N. and the
institutions of world order, but I believe that churches and synagogues should not only give strong support to the U.N. and to
efforts to improve its working; they should now put great stress

on the need for multilateral judgments upon American actions. The United States gets some support for its Asian policies from European allies and from nations on the eastern fringe of Asia, and doubtless it is always easy to find people around the world who are somewhat ambivalent because they see in the power of the United States the only countervailing power east of Suez. But let us not expect very much of this support and let us not allow it to lead to self-justification. Whatever anyone here may think of American policy to date in Vietnam, there is a terribly dangerous momentum in our power. We may easily become its prisoner. Also, the mounting of national self-justification may gradually cause the self-criticism that now exists to erode. There is danger that more complete moral isolation is not far away. Unless we find ways to submit our policies—policies that affect all mankind—to a far broader judgment than is now the case, we may become a nation possessed by a destructive determination to have our own way in Asia. Our religious communities are called to be an inner check on this development. This first inter-faith conference dealing with these issues should begin to prepare to meet this call.

5

Religion's Responsibility
to the Human Race

Rabbi Jacob J. Weinstein

Even after the Bible became an historically "finished" book, the Prophet's song of peace lingered on like a ghostly wraith over the still wide arena of man's barbarity to man. From the death of Bar Kochbah in the first century of the common era to the uprising of the few survivors of the Warsaw Ghetto—for some 1800 years— the Jew consistently turned the other cheek to the sword, and accepted the immolation of the *auto-da-fé* and became the chief victim of the Crusader. He knows in his blood and his bone the utter folly and futility of war. It is recidivist, infantile. He would apply the wisdom of Paul to the nations. When I was a child, I did as a child. When I grew up, I put away childish things. We are here, I trust, to further the intelligence of our democracy that we may become as a nation at least as mature as the more rationally educated individuals among us.

It is not easy to talk sense to power when that power is represented by a government still under the aegis of an unhappy mesalliance of national strategy and national obsession, of inept diplomacy and evangelical passions. It was calamity enough that brinkman Dulles foisted upon us the dubious policy of containment in that moment of agonizing reappraisal, but he added sorrow to injury when he served up this program with the fervor of a true believer in our nation's Manifest Destiny to be the global procurator of made-in-America democracy to all the heathen nations. It is often said that ministers of religion should stay out of politics. By the same token, should not ministers of state stay out of religion and leave conversion of the heathen to accredited missionaries? Yet, when one recognizes how inextricably interwoven are politics and religion; that, indeed, politics provides the focal points where religionists may inject their faith and vision into the stream of history, the question of *who* belongs *where* becomes irrelevant. What is relevant is that our statesmen hold to a high religion rather than to one that still echoes the frenzies of the "camp meeting."

And in no instance is that camp religion more primitive than in its insistence on making communism the behemoth bear and Communists the spawn of the Antichrist. This obsession with the Antichrist has given us little time and energy to serve God. It has corrupted our power to think calmly and sanely at a time when the ineluctable complexities of life make clear thinking not merely an intellectual delight but a condition of survival itself.

It is not hard to recall what a field day McCarthyism provided for the lunatic fringe in our country, and our more recent reappraisal of the "Communist threat." Today it seems incredible that a people could be thrown into panic on such flimsy evidence. Yet we are exhibiting that very same feeling of panic; only the places are different. So paranoid is our fear of communism still, that we cannot confront Caribbean, Asian, or African countries without proscribing not only Communists, but also Socialists, Anarchists, Syndicalists, Co-operators, Tolstoyans, Gandhists until we are constrained to relate only to active anti-Communists, who all too often are the feudal property owners, the remnants of the old ruling families and their loyal professional and civil servants. We seldom seek alliance with the kind of people we trust here; nor have we made any real effort to develop the kind of leadership that has made our country a truly magnificent social-welfare state. We play with the Bao Dais, Chang-kai-sheks, Batistas, Trujillos, Diems, Kys, and their confreres. We insist that our help be drained downward from the top in spite of formidable evidence that these elite suffer from faulty circulation and are rarely interested in sharing our generously conferred wealth. I have met African and Asian visitors who are amazed at the stark difference between the reality of a 90 per cent-realized democracy here and our fervid support of 95 per cent tyrannies abroad. In short, we put our worst foot forward. We export, it seems, the political and economic shibboleths we have discarded here. One sometimes gets the feeling that we have an inferiority complex about democracy's ability to confront totalitarian forms of government. The moment we are challenged, we whistle for the F.B.I. and the Marines. I suggest that we have more faith in the ultimate good sense of the people, here and abroad.

There is a poignant irony in the fact that we have a President who has done more in a shorter time to plug up the loopholes in our democracy than any other President and at the same time places the vast military powers of our government behind a foreign policy that seems intent on defeating or slowing down the very social revolution that brought this country to its high estate.

What but this obsession with communism prevents us from allowing people to choose a collective economy and a monolithic one-party system, believing as they do that time and the keener realization of the total needs of man will mellow collectivism into more permissive forms of co-operative life? Certainly they are as much entitled to believe this as that a state controlled by, and often the puppet of, a combination of generals and landowners will eventually mellow into a democratic polity. The fact is that the demands of human nature, the growth of education and the workings of an industrialized economy are creating certain conditions which largely determine the contour of political life. One has only to consider evidence from Russia and the satellite countries, from the Kibbutz movement in Israel, to realize that patterns of collectivism are not static but change into forms more congenial to individual needs.

The evidence is equally startling that the rugged individualism of the American frontier has shaped itself along various channels of social responsibility and community sharing. The tax power of our government is the great equalizer, and has produced a welfare state more socialistic in many aspects than anything Norman Thomas ever dreamed of. Wouldn't it be a tragedy if we blundered into an ideological war with China—a war that would inevitably force us to retreat from our war on poverty only to create those same conditions of poverty among the Chinese, freezing them into a bitter anti-Westernism and enslaving them forever to the passionate Trotskyism of Mao-tse-tung?

It is this same neurosis about communism that serves as the rationale for the stationing of our Seventh Fleet off the coast of China, the building of great air bases in Thailand and the islands off Japan, and then crying of bloody murder when the Chinese resent this threat to their security. Indeed, we think it unsporting of them to complain of the great big juicy bone of Taiwan we help keep lodged in their throat. The proverb says: "There is a way that seemeth right to a man but the ends thereof are the ways of death." We have long excused our acts of military aggression with the argument of U.S. "Operation Mercy": no sooner do we clear an area of Vietcong than we send in our mercy teams and build clinics, playgrounds, and vocational training shops, renew irrigation systems, and construct roads and bridges. I can testify that this work is done and done well by fine craftsmen and dedicated technicians. But I can also testify that its value is largely lost on the people, coming as it does in the wake of so much death and destruction. I recall visiting a village some twenty miles from Saigon which recently had been hit by a bomb intended for a Vietcong covert some miles from the village. I was in the company of a Cao-Daist monk and an interpreter provided by the psychological-warfare branch of our military. We both noticed a vegetable can lying in the debris with the legend: "A gift of the people of America to the people of Vietnam." The monk made a comment which the interpreter translated: "Neither your sting nor your honey. The right hand of your power destroys more than the left hand of your charity heals."

The Vietnamese are closely related to the Chinese. Their gentleness and sensitivity derive from the same cultural source. Buddhism is as alive in Vietnam as Confucianism and Taoism are in China. How is it, then, that we have failed so totally to consider the resistance these ancient religions will offer to a monolithic communism? I recall with special vividness the meeting a few of us, on the Emergency Clergyman's Committee for Vietnam, had with the venerable Tic Nat Hanh in a school house on the outskirts of Saigon. He first read to us from a letter he had written the previous April to Martin Luther King:

I believe with all my heart that the monks who burned
themselves did not aim at the death of the oppressors but
only at a change in their policy. Their enemies are not
man. They are intolerance, fanaticism, dictatorship, cu-
pidity, hatred and discrimination which lie at the heart
of man. I also believe with all my being that the struggle
for equality and freedom you lead in Birmingham, Ala-
bama . . . is not aimed at the whites but only at intolerance, hatred and discrimination. These are real enemies
of man—not man himself. In our unfortunate fatherland
we are trying to say desperately: do not kill man, even
in man's name. Please kill the real enemies of man which
are present everywhere, in our very hearts and minds.

Now in the confrontation of the big powers occurring
in our country, hundreds and perhaps thousands of Vietnamese peasants and children lose their lives every day,
and our land is unmercifully and tragically torn by a war
which is already twenty years old. I am sure that since
you have been engaged in one of the hardest struggles
for equality and human rights, you are among those who
understand fully, and who share with all their hearts, the
indescribable suffering of the Vietnamese people. The
world's greatest humanists would not remain silent. You
yourself cannot remain silent. America is said to have a
strong religious foundation, and spiritual leaders would
not allow American political and economic doctrines to
be deprived of the spiritual element. You cannot be silent
since you have already been in action and you are in action, too—to use Karl Barth's expression. And Albert
Schweitzer, with his stress on the reverence for life. And
Paul Tillich, with his courage to be, and thus, to love. . .

Nat Hanh thanked us for bringing a message from Dr. King
and went on to say that it was easier to find religious sympathy with
a dark-skinned leader, especially one who had given the world
the greatest demonstration of the effectiveness of non-violence. The
U.S. government, he went on, was confronting them with an un-
holy choice—that between communism and war—and he felt
that if this was the only choice he would be obliged to choose
communism, for he felt confident of his resources to combat and
triumph over communism. The ways of the Buddha cannot abide
the materialism, the determinism, the class-war violence of the

Communists. Let a Buddhist practice communism and the soul force of the Master's teaching, the 250 positive and negative commandments, will mold it into something quite different, something that neither Marx nor Mao-tse would ever recognize. But Buddhism cannot triumph over war. The violent death of war negates Nirvana. It accomplishes not the conscious liberation from the fever of desire but the annihilation of the very context in which desire and renunciation can operate. War uproots the four planes of Being and leaves only the chaos of destruction.

We get precious little of this understanding in our dialogue with China. Perhaps I am especially sensitive to this, as I was brought up in Portland, Oregon, and held a pulpit in San Francisco during the years of "the yellow peril" and knew the disparity between what the press said of the Chinese and what was in fact true. Apply the clichés of anti-communism on top of the "yellow peril" and you really come up with a nightmare. It is in this nightmare that we become callous and even brutal and reduce the Chinese—be he cooley or mandarin, peasant or poet—to a mere statistic. I heard a man in the New York subway gleefully saying to his neighbor: "Boy, the day is starting out fine. My I.B.M. stock went up six points, and we killed four hundred more Vietcong this week than last." As religionists, how can we permit the poison of propaganda or the passion of partisanship to erect a barrier between us and other sectors of the human family? I shall not soon forget that electric moment of bitter exchange between Madam Han Suyin, Chinese author and economist, and a member of our State Department at the conference on China held at the University of Chicago in March 1966. Mr. Halperin made a statement directed, it seemed, at Madam Suyin, that the "Chinese need take no comfort in the thought that if America uses a nuclear deterrent, only the urban Chinese will be hit. We can also get to your countryside." Madam Suyin became almost apoplectic as she shouted: "We are not afraid of your atom bomb—we are not afraid!" This incident was only one of several others that revealed our ineptness in dealing with China. It was readily apparent that our isolation from Red China, the ban on normal communication and interchange, was creating an abyss, the kind in which ignorant malice breeds and the normal human compassion that acts as a civilizing force between peoples is so easily eroded.

Now, in saying that a certain callousness and inhumanity has resulted from our policy in Vietnam, I do not mean to imply that those who support the government's position are callous and inhuman. Mr. Johnson and Mr. Humphrey, Ambassador Goldberg and Secretary of State Rusk, my Senator Paul Douglas and my Congressman Barrett O'Hara are as decent, civilized, generous, and sensitive human beings as any of us here. And certainly their intelligence and reasoning capacity are at least equal to the best of us here. What is therefore particularly disturbing is that these men can have such diverse positions. As servants of the government and trustees of what they believe to be the best interests of America, they believe most sincerely that what serves America best serves mankind best. They read out of history, or perhaps into history, the judgment that totalitarian regimes like those of nazism and communism must be stopped at some point. They believe that the failure to stop Hitler at Munich cost the world at least fifty million lives. They would rather sacrifice half a million Vietnamese and Allies now than pay the far heavier price later. They admit that this present war can be escalated into a nuclear war, but they hold China responsible for that risk. At the same time, they consider it better to take this risk than that of allowing the Communists to sweep into power all over the Far East.

It is here that we as religionists can perform our most useful role. We can work to counteract or modify the inevitable partisanship of those whose primary duty it is to protect the national interest. As servants of the Living God, our major responsibility is to the human race. As believers in the brotherhood of man, we must not permit the heady patriotism of war to demean that faith, to place national, racial, or creedal barriers between us and our fellow men. We must not allow the partisans of patriotism to alienate us from our yellow, black, or Communist brother to the extent that we consider him a different species of being unresponsive to the same fears and hopes that fill our hearts. Twice now in this century the organized religious community has failed to live up to this sacred responsibility. We dare not, if we would preserve faith as a resource of man, fail this time.

There are three major points in the preventive-war thesis with which we as men of religion must contend. First, let us grant for argument's sake the domino theory that the stand in Vietnam is necessary to preserve Laos, Cambodia, Thailand, Indonesia, Japan, and the Philippines; are we nevertheless morally justified in using the Vietnamese people as instruments, as laboratory guinea pigs in the testing of that theory? Do we have the right to impose that martyrdom on a people who have known some form of war or conquest for twenty-two years, a people who are desperately weary of war and beg only for the boon of peace? I cannot shake from my memory the plea of a young Vietnamese that if we must prove the superiority of containment over expansion, could we not choose another people and place for a change. It was only then, as I looked at what first appeared a young face, that I saw the fear in the deep of those brown eyes and the strain of corded neck muscles, the trembling of taut lips and the horror of the years of death and destruction which had dogged him from his cradle to this very day. How can any religious person accept the proposition that a people without their consent can be used to test even the noblest experiment?

Second, as to the automatic inevitability of the domino theory: Cambodia, Thailand, Burma, and Indonesia have managed to resist the Communists, not merely because of French or American intervention, but because there are viable alternatives for these people, a sophisticated people who know the difference between freedom and order and who are subtle in their knowledge of the various ways to combine both with justice and peace.

Third, a military defeat of the Vietcong will not necessarily open the way either for a democratic form of government or for one more congenial to the United States. It is just as possible that the Vietcong will be driven underground and that any viable government will be possible only by maintaining a vast police force—a task that is already straining our resources in other parts of the world.

Last, it seems improbable that any kind of peace can be arranged without recognizing the National Liberation Front as a most important component of the negotiating team. Ho-chi-minh is criminally wrong in insisting that the NLF be the only negotiator, but we are equally wrong in excluding them either before or after a properly supervised election. Indeed, the failure to include the Vietcong is tantamount to saying that we want to turn the government over to the army colonels. Various suggestions for

peaceful alternatives will be made in other papers. We plead only
that we recognize in the peoples of Vietnam, North and South,
and in the peoples of China members of the family of man possessed of the same hopes and fears as we are.

6

The Role of Arms in the Search for Peace

Arthur W. Barber

In his book *The Sleepwalkers,* Arthur Koestler suggests that great steps forward in astronomy were made in an intuitive and mystic, rather than a logical, fashion; specifically that many of the concepts put forward by Copernicus were correct conclusions drawn from erroneous data and irrelevant arguments. I have the feeling that, today, the human society, like Copernicus, is moving in the right direction, but that many of the arguments may be irrelevant. Too many intellectuals and policy-makers believe that the motivation of men's deeds is all-important; that if our objectives are sound and high-principled, so must be the realization of those objectives, and, by the same token, that selfish motives beget poor deeds. Yet, looking back along the long road of history, who can imagine or understand the motivation that led Sparta and Athens to destroy each other, or Metternich's motives in formulating the Treaty of Vienna, which provided peace for the European community for over a century? Foreign policy cannot be debated on some abstract level in which the motivations of one side or another are constantly, and uselessly, held up for examination. History will judge the wisdom of our acts, not by our motives, but by the consequences of our deeds.

What does religion have to contribute to foreign policy? To

those who would say "Nothing," I disagree. I suggest that religious
and ethical beliefs shape our views of the world in which we live.
If religious values are not an operative factor in international relations today, it is because too many human beings have drawn an
artificial division between morality, politics, and policy. In the past
century, nationalism has caused a breach between morality and
politics. What is required is once again to attempt to think through
our political ethics. Religion should provide the basis of one's concept of political community.

It is first of all necessary to recognize the distinction between
the concept of community and that of society; the distinction between a neighbor and a good neighbor. The members of a community assist one another, while members of some self-centered
societies do not. This distinction is essential if we are to understand
the missing elements in a more rational world, for, as society becomes ever more organized, and men are engineered, calculated,
and self-divided to provide a more effective increasing productiv-
ity, individuals become ever more fragmented.

The moral options of our time depend upon our concepts of
ourselves and the role of the individual in our society. Once we
forget that every man is an object of concern for the sole reason
that he is a human being, the destruction of civilization becomes
merely a question of time.

As the forces that affect men's lives originate with men, so the
problems created by men can be solved by men. Johnson or Kosy-
gin, Mao-tse-tung or de Gaulle—each is a product of his age, his
experience, and his intellectual environment. Among world leaders
and individual citizens, political pressures, old habits and customs
stand in the way of adaptation to a new world. We are only beginning to understand new ways of using our intelligence in order to
preserve and expand the opportunities for the human species. In
this effort, the best of every man and woman is needed.

As participants in the evolution of the human community, we
must also recognize the major role played by religion.

Between 4000 and 3000 B.C., in the fertile lands between the
Tigris and the Euphrates, the priests of Sumeria persuaded their
people that man was a slave to the gods, created to free the gods
and their representatives, the priests, from the necessity of work.
On this basis, human civilization began 5,000 years ago.

As long as the cities along the rivers were small, and undeveloped areas lay between them, life followed a fixed sacred and relatively peaceful routine, but when the cities expanded and impinged on each other, wars broke out and armies were needed for defense. The result was the creation of the first professional armies and the concept of kingships: military leaders who assumed temporal power. By 2500 B.C. military alliances were formed about the cities of Lagash and Umma. At this time the gods and their priests depended upon the king for both military protection and economic support, and so now the gods of the city did battle with one another, cursing one's enemies and praising one's friends.

Thus, from the beginning of history, man's search for God, and for personal significance, has all too often led to war. As Dostoevsky wrote in *The Brothers Karamazov*:

> So long as man remains free he strives for nothing so incessantly and so painfully as to find someone to worship. But man seeks to worship what is established beyond dispute, so that all men would agree at once to worship it. For these pitiful creatures are concerned not only to find what one or the other can worship, but to find something that all would believe in and worship: what is essential is that all men be together in it. This craving for community of worship is the chief misery of every man individually and of all humanity from the beginning of time. For the sake of common worship they've slain each other with the sword. They have set up gods and challenged one another, "Put away your gods and come and worship ours or we will kill you and your gods!"

Until 1400 the nations of Europe thought of themselves as one society. While wars and religious schisms regularly occurred, the Christian world recognized itself as one. The schisms within the Catholic Church at no time brought into question the concept held by laymen as well as clergy that all Christians ought to try to live together under the laws of God. Documents of the day frequently referred to the concept of the Christian commonwealth: *res publica Christiana*. This Christian commonwealth was no mere abstraction, for by this time it had developed the foundations of what we now call international law. In canon law, the Catholic Church brought about a synthesis of Christian morals, feudal customs, and

Roman legal thought. Canon law, in turn, supplied the basis for international law. This derived not so much from formal statutes or treaties as from generally accepted principles or old established customs of the Christian world. The religious and ethical rules for a great international society were sacrificed to the secular allegiance demanded by the nation-state.

Some time after 1400, international relations took a dramatic turn. At that time the disputes among the popes led to the establishment of the first amoral sovereign states. As in ancient Mesopotamia, the land in upper Italy was becoming completely organized —the gaps between city-states were narrowing—and, as a result of the increasing pressure, warfare broke out more regularly. However, the business-minded citizens of the secular city-states, such as Venice, were not interested in war. They, to an increasing extent, left the actual fighting to professional soldiers. Wars waged by mercenaries under generals jealous of their equipment and men tended to be far less bloody and decisive than the earlier clashes between citizen militias. As war became more rational, less glorious, and more civilized, success depended upon negotiation rather than battle, and modern professional diplomacy was born. The first permanent ambassadors were the papal representatives established at this time.

The Thirty Years' War led to the creation of the modern nation-state throughout Europe. This religiously inspired holocaust, which devastated Central Europe and resulted in 30 million deaths, persuaded men on both sides to recognize the necessity of law and reason.

Unfortunately, this step toward the rule of reason was largely negated by the concurrent evolution of the nation-state—ruled by its people rather than by the aristocracy. For most of recorded history, the sovereignty and power of the nation-state was based upon the concept of the God-given omnipotent power of kings. The aristocracy, while they pursued their personal interests in a quite cold-blooded manner, nevertheless restrained their military forces, albeit for economic rather than humanitarian reasons: they did not wish to lose materiel or men unnecessarily. Thus, rationalists like Grotius and Clausewitz would argue for the principle of economy of force. As Grotius said:

All damage done to the enemy unnecessarily, every act of hostility which does not tend to procure victory and bring the war to a conclusion, is a licentiousness condemned by the law of nature.

Rousseau and Locke held to the belief, which was eventually widely accepted, that according to God's natural law, power belonged to the people. And, in some mystical fashion, the God-given power of right and wrong had passed to the popular majority, who could do no wrong.

This philosophical view was translated into policy when the basis for the popular nation-state was laid by the French Revolution in 1796. The outlines of total war could be seen in the memorandum of the directoire of the revolution, which mobilized every citizen of the French state to serve the French army in the name of the popular will—an act of which no monarch would have dreamed:

All Frenchmen are permanently requisitioned for service in the armies.

The young men shall fight; the married men shall forge weapons and transport supplies, the women will make tents and clothes and will serve in the hospitals; the children will make up old linen into lint; the old men will have themselves carried into the public square to arouse the courage of the fighting men, to preach the unity of the republic and hatred against kings.

When Napoleon's forces were destroyed by the alignment of the aristocracy of Europe, the Vienna peace settlement represented a clear, if only temporary, victory for reason. While conservatism and skillful private diplomacy are targets of popular criticism, I for one admire in retrospect Metternich's attempt in 1815 to organize Europe according to the principles of law and restraint. This rational world created by the Treaty of Vienna did not exist for long, for the revolutions of 1848 shook the framework of aristocracy and legitimacy, creating a period in which nationalism and the popular will were openly exalted at the expense of the law. These popular revolutions directly led to the nihilism of nationalism. Paradoxically, they were supported neither by the radical left nor right, but by the liberal parties of the middle class. Nationalism was the religion of the nineteenth century and few, if any, were non-believers. Engels, one of the founders of communism, conducted a fervent national campaign against the liberation of Poland.

The Industrial Revolution was to provide nationalism with the technological foundation for total war, as dramatically illustrated by the Civil War. Compare the opening battles at Bull Run, conducted in the tradition of the European armies of an aristocratic pre-industrial age, with the trench warfare of Petersburg, where use of rapid-fire rifle and cannon made for a war not dissimilar from World Wars I or II or Korea.

One of the vital questions of our time is whether last year, which represented the 100th anniversary of the end of the Civil War, will also represent the end of a century of total war.

If it is to do so, we must find our way between abstract idealism and irresponsible cynicism or existentialism. The concept of the idealist who stands apart from the crisis of his times is not new. After the Peloponnesian War, confusion, violence, and irrational behavior characterized the Greek state. Thucydides described the situation as follows:

> . . . The politicians on each side were armed with high sounding slogans. . . . Both boasted that they were servants of the community and both made the community the prize of war. The only purpose of their policy was the extermination of their opponents, and to achieve this they stopped at nothing. Where no contract or obligation was binding, nothing could heal the conflict, and since security was only to be found in the assumption that nothing was secure, everyone took steps to preserve himself and no one could afford to trust his neighbor. . . .

Plato advised the lover of justice to

> . . . remain quietly at his own work like a traveler caught in a storm who retreats behind a wall to shelter from the driving gusts of dust and hail. Seeing the rest of the world filled full of iniquity, he will be content to keep his own life on earth untainted by wickedness and impious actions, so that he may leave this world with a fair hope of the next, at peace with himself and God.

The results of the division between abstract idealism and irresponsible cynicism can perhaps best be illustrated by U.S. policy following World War I. In 1919, in a speech in which he unsuccessfully sought the support of the American people to save the League of Nations, President Wilson called upon the American people to leave

> . . . the mists that lie close to the ground, getting upon strong wing into those upper spaces of the air where you can see with a clear eye the affairs of mankind, see how the affairs of America are linked with the affairs of men everywhere, see how the world turns with outstretched hands to this blessed country of ours and says, "If you will lead, we will follow."

But the American people were not willing to follow. They were unwilling to meet their responsibilities as a world power, and the League of Nations failed. Strangely enough, the popular view was articulated well by Wilson's military advisor, General Tasker H. Bliss, who at that time wrote privately:

> What a wretched mess it all is: If the rest of the world will let us alone, I think we better stay on our side of the water and keep alive the spark of civilization to relight the torch after it is extinguished over here. If I ever had any illusions, they are all dispelled.

Fortunately, new forces are abroad in the world which do not support either the blind passions of ideology or the irresponsible withdrawal from the world. If we are to create a world of justice, law, and order, the light of reason is required—nothing more and nothing less.

In the great industrial nations of the world, which are the only ones that have the power to launch a nuclear war, there is a new caution and respect for reality. While irrational behavior and violence receive publicity, the quiet victories of reason are daily shaping a brighter future.

When Dean Rusk was recently asked what he regarded the most important achievement of his four years in office, he said: "We have promoted general recognition that nuclear war cannot be used as an instrument of policy."

While it is less clear, it also seems that traditional, conventional aggression such as occurred under Hitler in Europe, Tojo in the Pacific, and the Communists in Korea may well be a thing of the past. This leaves two major unfulfilled tasks before the world community: the effective control of revolutions directed and conducted from external sources such as we now face in Vietnam and elsewhere in underdeveloped countries, and world-wide limitations upon the spread of nuclear weapons.

The challenge of revolutions directed and conducted from external sources has been demonstrated during the past year in South Vietnam. The North Vietnamese and the National Liberation Front, supported and encouraged by the Chinese Communists, attempted to launch an all-out drive to destroy the army of South Vietnam and bring down its government. Not only was the infiltration of men and supplies from North Vietnam into South Vietnam accelerated; regular units of the North Vietnamese army were brought in for the attack. The U.S. government had made it known for many years that it would view with the greatest concern any Communist attempt to seize the territory of South Vietnam by force of arms. Our response to that threat was exactly what the aggressors should have anticipated: we promptly came to the aid of the people of South Vietnam with the forces needed to halt the attack and throw it back. We have said time and time again that we would do everything necessary to help these people defend their freedom and independence as long as they themselves were willing to carry on the struggle.

We have shouldered this heavy burden for several reasons: First, we believe that the people of South Vietnam, like people everywhere, should have the right to decide their own destiny. Second, we intend to honor our commitment to help defend the people of South Vietnam, just as we will honor our defense commitments to other nations. Third, peace cannot be gained by permitting aggression to succeed. However, the responsibility for deterring and meeting Communist aggression is not ours alone. Other countries can and should bear their share of the burden and play an active role in the search for peace and the constructive enterprises that can and must accompany it. We must be constantly alert to new opportunities to build the kind of international political institutions that will permit peaceful constructive growth, while thwarting terrorism and destruction.

Even while we, together with our friends and allies, continue the struggle in Southeast Asia, we hold open wide the door to a just settlement of that conflict. President Johnson and Secretary Rusk have restated in a hundred different ways our willingness to move that conflict from the battlefield to the conference table. The position of the U.S. government on peace in Vietnam, as most recently outlined by Secretary of State Rusk, is as follows:

1. The Geneva Agreements of 1954 and 1962 are an adequate basis for peace in Southeast Asia;

2. We would welcome a conference on Southeast Asia or on any part thereof;

3. We would welcome "unconditional discussions," as President Johnson put it;

4. A cessation of hostilities could be the first order of business at a conference or could be the subject of preliminary discussions;

5. Hanoi's four points could be discussed along with other points others might wish to propose;

6. We want no U.S. bases in Southeast Asia;

7. We have no desire to retain U.S. troops in South Vietnam after peace is assured;

8. We support free elections in South Vietnam to give the South Vietnamese a government of their own choice;

9. The question of reunification of Vietnam should be determined by the Vietnamese through their own free decision;

10. The countries of Southeast Asia can be non-aligned or neutral if that be their option;

11. We would much prefer to use our resources for the economic reconstruction of Southeast Asia than for war. If there is peace, North Vietnam could participate in a regional effort to which we would be prepared to contribute at least one billion dollars;

12. The President has said, "The Vietcong would not have difficulty being represented and having their views represented if for a moment Hanoi decided she wanted to cease aggression. I don't think that would be an insurmountable problem";

13. We have said publicly and privately that we could stop the bombing of North Vietnam as a step toward peace, although there has not been the slightest hint or suggestion from the other side as to what they would do if the bombing stopped.

Thus, the continuation of the conflict is not our choice but, rather, the choice of our adversaries. It will be terminated when they are convinced that their aggression cannot succeed, and when they reach that conclusion, I am sure they will find no difficulty in communicating their intentions to us.

Nonproliferation

At the same time we must attempt to gain international acceptance on limitations of nuclear weapons. The President's January 1966 message to the Eighteen-Nation Disarmament Conference reflects the commitment of the U.S. government to stop the spread of nuclear weapons:

> The avoidance of war and particularly nuclear war is the central common concern of all mankind.

> My country is dedicated to this end. The effort to control, and reduce—and ultimately eliminate—modern engines of nuclear destruction is fundamental to our policy. We have, with all mankind, a common interest in acting now to prevent nuclear spread, to halt the nuclear-arms race, and to reduce nuclear stocks.

The President drew attention to the resolutions introduced in both houses of Congress endorsing the administration's program to prevent the spread of nuclear weapons, citing them as "an indication of the importance that the people of the United States attribute to such measures. . ." and adding that he fully shared these views.

It is of prime importance that we have clear in our minds ways in which we and other nations can work together to stop nuclear spread. To this end, our task is the creation of international restraints and an international climate that would make it possible for these countries to decide for themselves that the acquisition of nuclear weapons is not in their national interests.

This difficult task cannot be achieved by the United States alone. And it will not be achieved in any single agreement on nonproliferation, although such an agreement would certainly make a valuable contribution to our objective. A treaty against nuclear proliferation imposes important legal, moral, and political restraints upon the signatories. However, if a country is faced with a situation in which it believes that possession of nuclear weapons is essential to preserve its vital interests, international treaties are but one factor on the scales of decision.

In our efforts to develop an effective nonproliferation program, certain obstacles concerning safeguards and protection have arisen. We strongly support the establishment of international safeguards under the International Atomic Energy Agency for all peaceful atomic programs. We have made significant progress in gaining international acceptance, and have placed the atomic reactor at Rowe and other U.S. reactors under the international-safeguards program. We hope that those nations that have not accepted safeguards will do so.

As time goes by, the question of multilateral assurances on the part of nuclear states to non-nuclear states must be resolved. We must continue to try to work out with other nuclear powers appropriate arrangements to guarantee non-nuclear states against nuclear attack. Certainly these states will want—and deserve—some assurances of protection against either nuclear attack or even large-scale conventional attack if they give up the right to acquire weapons.

Ultimately the U.N. or some other multilateral body will be faced with the problem. The President has stated very clearly that we will support non-nuclear powers who do not acquire nuclear weapons against threats of nuclear blackmail. Exactly how that guarantee will be translated into detailed terms will no doubt be a subject for further discussion by the U.N. and other powers.

The request of the non-nuclear powers that the nuclear powers limit or reduce the level of inventories of nuclear weapons is one to which we must give serious consideration.

Success in the endeavor to limit nuclear arms is essential if the peoples of the world are "to establish justice, insure domestic tranquility, provide for the common defense, promote the general welfare, and secure the blessings of liberty to ourselves and our posterity."

Today, we are living on the brink of an extraordinary future. Our children may someday look back at this period as the first blind, fumbling, but instinctive steps toward a new world of politics and social values—a world in which traditional attitudes may be singularly irrelevant. President Johnson has said:

These are the most hopeful times in all the years since Christ was born. As never before, man has in his possession the capacities to end war and preserve peace, to eradicate poverty and share abundance, to overcome the diseases that have afflicted the human race and permit all mankind to enjoy their promise in life on this earth.

This future of high promise is not merely desirable; it is possible. And as it will be determined by men, not machines, so it will be fashioned, not by the quantity of our atomic stockpile, but by the quality of our society and the convictions of its citizens.

I welcome the high motives and good intentions which have led to this National Inter-Religious Conference on peace. Your advice and your efforts will be welcomed by your government, not only now, but at any time in the future. Only through such constructive co-operation can we work together to build the kind of world we all desire.

7

Peace Is More Than a Word

Vice President Hubert H. Humphrey

I am a man of peace. My life has been devoted to it. I am not a military man. My greatest military experience was with a Boy Scout troop. I am very deeply interested in freedom, in self-determination, and in a world of law and order. I have never believed that we should tolerate aggression, whether it is in a city, in a nation, or between nations.

I was a mayor of a city. We had a good city. Even though I attended church regularly, even though we mobilized the churches of our city, even though we had Prayer Sunday, Police Sunday, and Order Sunday, we not only had to use the police department; we had to double the size of it. But we built a good city. We passed the first fair-employment ordinance; had housing legislation; cleaned up our city slums and tried to do something about a better community. This is the kind of world I believe we ought to live in —a world of better communities.

I worked with young people a good deal and I still do. As the father of some young people, I am worried about them and their future. I can tell you that not only do I worry; your President worries also. There is not one of us who has not a heavy heart in these difficult days. What man with the slightest bit of compassion can bear to see people die, see their young lives snuffed out, and see the patterns of brutality and cruelty spread across the pages of our press, reminding people of the heartache of war?

I have respect for different people's points of view. I read only recently an article in which I was cited as having said that dissent threatened our security. I had to write the author of that column a rather firm note, not merely because he quoted me incorrectly, but because it is my firm conviction that the sacred right of dissent is one of the things that we are really fighting for, if one wishes to put it in those words. I believe in freedom of choice; I believe in the right of people to be different. I believe that freedom means the right to dissent as well as the right to advocate. This is a precious right. Even if we knew that what people were dissenting about was wrong, it would still be wrong to deny them that right. There is an evil to cutting off dissent.

In sixteen years in Congress I conducted a few inquiries and asked a few pointed questions. I do it yet. As a member of the Foreign Relations Committee from 1952 to 1964, I did some work on the test-ban treaty and on disarmament. When no one thought we could pass the test-ban treaty—and some present here were involved—we thought we could pass it and we did it. And we haven't given up that struggle for peace yet.

Despite the differences of opinion concerning the Declaration of Honolulu, a great part of that declaration embodied what I have been working for within this government, what others have been working for, and what our President wanted. Believe it or not, even in the government we have differences of opinion. We express those differences freely and openly; indeed, if we fail to express them, we are encouraged to do so by the President himself. I have sat in meetings where the President has, in the face of too much unanimity, appointed what is called a devil's advocate, one expected to argue the position as thoroughly as possible. There are no yes-men, only people who try to think through problems and work from a body of evidence. We may draw conclusions with which the public does not agree, but there is an honest effort made to draw the right conclusions. I know of not a single person who is a warmonger.

I have heard a lot about doves and hawks, but I just don't think we are birds. We are human beings. I have heard a lot about liberals and conservatives; yet, some of the most conservative people I have heard are against our even being in Vietnam, while some of the most liberal are for increasing our forces there. I find people who are identified with one group or another, but I don't think we make judgments as liberals or conservatives, doves or hawks. Rather, we make judgments on the basis of our own feelings, our own values, our own information, our own commitments, and our dedication. I think we ought to respect each other's judgments.

I want you to know that, as Vice President, as a member of the National Security Council and of the President's Cabinet, my office is open to you and your representatives any time you want to meet. You need never feel for a single day or minute that any door is closed to you. The President of the United States would not want any door closed to you. If you can't find me in the Executive Office Building, try the Capitol. I generally put in a pretty long day, so if you don't find me early in the morning or late in the afternoon, you can find me late at night. Here I am right now, at a rather late hour.

I say to you—quite frankly—that I look forward to meeting your leadership, your representatives, or whatever delegation you wish to send. We always want to visit with you and learn from you. Maybe in the exchange of views there will be more common denominators than you believe there are at the present moment. I believe there will be much we will see in common in terms of trying to build a new life for billions of people.

We Americans claim to be world leaders, but we have only half a world of knowledge. We are very well educated about Europe, slightly informed about Latin America, but abysmally ignorant about Asia and Africa. We can't be a full world leader and a world power with half a world of knowledge. This is why I have so strongly endorsed the hearings that are under way with reference to the study of China and Asia. You know what I have said. We must keep the door open for intelligent thinking about Asia on the part of this government for the future.

You have the luxury of independence of action and thought. I have responsibilities. You don't have to weigh every word and every measure as I do, not in terms of our associates, but in terms of other governments and other problems around the world. Thus it is not quite as easy for me as it was when I was in the Senate. Now I have to think about what I say, and what I don't say, not only because of how it is interpreted here at home, but also because of how it is received abroad. It doesn't take very much intelligence to start an international fight or to create misunderstandings, but it does take a little to prevent one and to be able to bring understanding.

I am going to try to do my best to work for what I believe to be a just peace, to work for what I believe to be a world of law and order, a world in which the law of the jungle has no place, a world in which people set their sights upon helping to build a better life. We have had the fuss and fury over the struggle in Vietnam, Thailand, Laos, and Cambodia. I was there, on the Mekong River; I've seen the poverty, the distress, and we have got to do something about it. Not that we can do it alone; we can't. Not that we should; but we can help. The only way we are going to be able to help is for people in America to understand that it is a part of their business. They must understand that this is a mighty small world, as small as the astronauts have made it, as small as modern communication has made it. Today it takes less time to fly from Washington to Saigon than it did from Washington to Berlin twenty-five years ago: yet, now the nation that finds itself willing to rise up in arms to the defense of Berlin argues over other matters.

I am a peace man—so are you. Sometimes it is difficult to believe, the way we argue, but let's try to work together. I assure you that I want to work with you.

The noblest achievement of mankind, the ultimate goal of civilization, is peace—more than a word, more than the absence of war. Peace is a positive force, and it takes a long time to get it. It's almost like the building of a mighty cathedral—a wonderful great temple that takes a plan, a master plan, an architect, a master architect, and the labors of many. You build it block by block and sometimes generations upon generations. It doesn't come mysteriously or magically. The peace we seek to build is not only the end to hostilities, but also a time of health and education, of jobs and work, of families and shelter, of communities, of a wholesome environment and opportunity. The peace we seek is one free of prejudice and discrimination and all the evil things we know and have worked against. That is the peace we seek.

8

The Will for Peace

Bishop John J. Wright

Sister Thomasine, who has here been so frequently quoted by friendly rabbis and genial bishops, remarked that the only thing especially significant and permanently important about this conference is the fact that it *is* inter-religious. It serves as an example of ecumenical action on a level and in an area of moral concern where no one doubts either the desirability or the possibility of ecumenically shared witness, planning, and action.

This historic fact is more than enough justification for the fatigue and sense of partial frustration inevitable at the end of a meeting so complex and seeking objectives so elusive. In this regard, it also seems only fitting to say that almost everything we have attempted to do together in these few days has, in fact, been better done by our respective individual religious groups, having enjoyed much more time than we have had, and setting for themselves less complicated purposes than we—generously, perhaps, but somewhat ingenuously—set for ourselves in projecting this parley. We have not only tried to "unscrew" the inscrutable, but we have done so with teams made up of people who had never worked together under the same union jurisdiction or on the same job.

These several days have found us working together for the first time in a common effort to arrive at a common conscience in the light of commonly shared principles brought to bear on problems of peace and war which shock us with common concern. Moreover, we have provided a common forum, the scope and agenda of which can grow with further sharing of ideas, to the great good of both religion and the cause of peace. This forum has functioned within our workshops, and the reports issuing from these are offered as tentative findings from the honest discussions of specific problems on which we find ourselves divided in particular applications even when we may be largely agreed in principle.

We have nevertheless established, once and for all, a pattern for inter-religious co-operation in creating a moral climate for peace. I find it an encouraging omen that, as we were launching our religious project here in Washington, another launching was taking place at Cape Kennedy, a launching undertaken with dedication to peace no less passionate than ours and with frustrations no less painful. The arrival of the Space Age imposes on us the obligation to make quite certain that, in a world now well aware that E equals MC^2 and prepared to implement all the scientific corollaries of this basic formula, we who speak for religion arrive at moral formulas equally clear, and that we bring to the practical corollaries of our agreed moral formulas a determination programmed as is that of the world of science. It is significant that something went wrong in the world of technology during these same days, and that obviously there is a considerable amount of work to be done before the space ships, which will play so great a part in the peace of the future, can function as effectively as they are intended to do. It should not, therefore, either discourage or scandalize us if our moral formulas are not functioning smoothly, to the satisfaction of all present. It is a gratification in the case of both the launch-off into space and the discussions here that we are able to make, discover, reconsider, and correct our mistakes in public.

For these reasons, I conclude that the peace parley has been a success, going beyond two possible patterns within which it might have been unhappily limited: (1) a peace rally or demonstration long on earnestness but short on ideas; (2) a pleasant symposium bringing together once again good friends who have been meeting to agree with one another these twenty years and more (to my knowledge and personal edification), serious but long known partisans of peace.

Thank God this parley finds these stalwarts still at work, but there are many new faces on the scene and many new hands in the work! Permit me also to note, with a certain bemusement all will share this week, the mounting fierceness of the Friends, the implacable intransigence of the Fellowship of Reconciliation, and the amazing trend toward peaceful ways among the Irish, give or take the blowing up of a monument or two when there is no danger of anyone's being killed!

In its substantial thrust, our parley has not departed from the basic purpose spelled out when Dr. Greeley and Rabbi Eisendrath, both appealing to the call of Pope John XXIII in *Pacem in Terris*, first brought us together. That purpose was exemplified by Pope Paul VI in his speech to the U.N. and underscored by Pope Paul VI when, in his recent talk to the diplomatic corps accredited to the Holy See, he said: "When the Church does preach principles concerning peace and war, she is heard with respect. Her opinion is awaited and even sought out."

We have had the Holy Father's conviction confirmed by the cordial and repeated interest of U Thant, Secretary General of the U.N., and by the message from the President of the United States, urging us not to content ourselves with any vague "quest for peace" but to bear our moral witness in the most forthright and specific fashion. This same openness to the voice of religion was no small part of Vice President Humphrey's motivation in appearing at our parley.

Consistent with this understanding of the necessary and proper role of religion in its moral witness within the political order, our agreed intent was and remains, not to second-guess diplomats or sit in judgment on heads of states, but to do our own job as spokesmen for religion. That job, specifically ours, is one that governments desperately need but badly complicate when they interfere with it. I refer to the job of creating a moral climate that gives the hope and the chance of organic life to the otherwise dead, merely mechanical organized structures for peace that diplomats and statesmen devise and blueprint. The organization of the world for peace is the business of those who have in their hands the instruments and on their consciences the responsibilities of the temporal order; the organic spirit that gives life, unity, and direction to that work, even in its temporal aspects, depends largely on how those who preach moral goodness, social truth, and ethical beauty meet their religious obligations. The expectation that both jobs be done in all-out, urgent fashion by the respective representatives of both church and state corresponds to an increasingly insistent and universal demand of men everywhere.

Cardinal Ottaviani, in a justly acclaimed speech at the Ecumenical Council, went so far as to say that that council "should give its vote to the creation of one world republic composed of all the nations of the world in which no longer would there be strife among various nations, but an entire world living in peace." The Cardinal went on to appeal to that "peace of Christ in the reign of Christ" in which he sees no small part of the hope of such peace.

Many of us would probably not be prepared to go as far as the Cardinal. But all are agreed that the most imperative task of honest diplomacy in the service of the common good has now become the organization of all the world for peace. We would agree, too, that such an organization requires and presupposes some organic principle, and that such a principle must necessarily be moral. Hence, the function of religion, of all religion worthy of the name in our day, must include the fostering of that life-principle of the needed moral atmosphere, the creation of an organic climate for peace without which organization becomes merely mechanical. In fact, in the absence of such an organic moral soul, any merely organized unity becomes not only mechanical but in all probability despotically destructive of the personal and community values that all society, regional or international, exists to serve.

In the absence of such a moral climate, political and diplomatic structures for peace operate in a vacuum, and so can only disintegrate. Unfortunately, organized efforts at world peace have too often been the object of the same indifference as, innocently enough in its case, surrounds organizations like the International Postal Union. In the case of the Postal Union, the relative absence of moral idealism warming its operation is probably not so important. But the prolonged absence of intense moral interest in and religious support of the organization of the world for peace and for the development of the human good has been disastrous, indeed scandalous. It is the supreme purpose of this parley to put an end to that scandal at least so far as religion in America is concerned.

Pope Paul's visit to the U.N. during its critical anniversary year, the growing participation of all religious groups in U.N. and related programs, this very parley on religion and peace—all are historic signs of the times and provide encouraging evidence that the organization of world peace may now receive a dynamic, organic moral principle of life and growth.

One especially hopes that churchmen will put their best brains and most ardent hearts in the formulation of a positive theology of peace. The relative dearth of such a theology is again a grave scandal; surely here we have an ecumenical task to do.

The responsibilities of religious spokesmen to questions of peace and war are heightened by the fact that religious differences, in many cases, have more than once been among the contributing factors in the rise of international conflicts and the waging of war. We need not comb the history of the Middle Ages, the Crusades, the Old Testament, or the ancient world for specific examples. Even in the modern world, the exploitation of religious feelings as between Moslems and Hindus in the problem of Kashmir, the mutual distrust between some Christians and some Buddhists in Southeast Asia, the heritage of incompatibility between Jews and Moslems in the Near East, the role of religious antagonism between Christians and Moslems in areas like Cyprus, prove that religion can be and often is a factor in the appeal to war.

It is not enough to exorcise any antique concept of "holy war." It is imperative to make quite certain that in modern times religious idealism is on guard against the use of religious emotion as a factor in promoting war.

The "war on war" proclaimed by Pope Pius XII, the program of "peace on earth" outlined by Pope John XXIII, the pleas for "war no more, no more war" by Pope Paul VI—all presuppose that the only "holy war" permitted to believers in God in our day is the crusade to build peace and that the energies of religious emotion, as well as religious idealism, must henceforth be entirely on the side of the forces that build just and enduring peace.

In this connection, some honest talk is not only in order but should be welcomed by every side. Pope John's oft-quoted Italian word, *aggiornamento,* which has entered into the *lingua franca* of all nations (together with *Pacem in Terris*), has not only the sense of "updating" usually attributed to it, but a dictionary sense of "stocktaking" or "balancing our books." On the basis of these definitions, our primary purpose should be to set our own houses in order, making quite certain that we are doing our proper job of preaching peace before we presume either to criticize the jobs of others or to venture technical suggestions of our own. This is particularly true in the very areas that have found us, in varying degrees, divided among ourselves within this parley. Such differences (inevitable and healthy because they give a dynamic to the sifting of our evidence, the weighing of our motives, and the purification of our principles) should increase our sense of responsible discretion in the choice of the words we use to evaluate or label the honest judgments or even fears of others than ourselves. This is especially true in the delicate matter of dealing for the first time with Communist regimes; it is also true in the effort to arrive at accurate and normative readings of the history of American efforts to promote or preserve the peace.

Differences in our readings of these matters will be inevitable and well-founded. Believers must prepare themselves for present and future constructive dialogue with the world of honest unbelievers, the Communist world included. We must always review with special moral vigilance the peace record of our own land and all the groups to which we give our own loyalties.

Some of us may not, however, always come up with the same choice of words to express the values involved. I, for example, must admit that my ear, if not my eyebrow, went up a bit at the choice of one word by our so eloquent, sensitive, and reliable keynoter, Dr. John C. Bennett. I agree that people can be "obsessed" by communism, as they can be obsessed by anything else. I agree that "obsession" is always unhealthy; when present, it calls for psychiatric, rather than spiritual, attention. But I am not sure that the word "obsession" is accurate to describe the fears of communism among most people in the religious and even democratic world. That such a fear exists, however it is described, warrants neither pessimism nor negativism on the part of believers with regard to the dialogue with unbelievers and to the positive results to be hoped for from that dialogue. But a realism is needed to keep us from having the gentleness of the dove while lacking that wisdom of the serpent which the Divine Teacher linked to His counsel concerning the conduct of "doves."

The wisdom which the Scriptures bid us to attain was born of experience, sometimes tragic. It is a wisdom born of reason, sometimes stumbling. It is a wisdom that has been constantly subject to growth, above all in problems of war and peace, from the days of Plato and his Fair City, from the days of the Hebrew "blessed vision of peace," through the days of the City of God and the City of Man, of Dante's *De Monarchia*, through the grand designs of the eighteenth and nineteenth centuries, to the dreams of the U.N. and perhaps even of a world republic destined to be.

The wisdom that we are meant to develop has far different roots from that of the serpent, but we must make quite sure that we do not eschew that wisdom. We are persuaded that human, if not indeed divine, forces operate to relieve the monolithic structure of totalitarian institutions, including those of Marxist inspiration, and to tame the fury of crude Communist class and other violence. We believe that basic human realities (such as those so well developed by the keynote speakers, specifically Dr. Bennett) make the break-down of any totalitarianism and any monolith inevitable. Naturally this involves important questions of timing and of tactic about which some will have their legitimate differences of opinion; I am confident that, as this entire conference is at one with Dr. Bennett in his basic hope, it will also be at one with some of us in our reservations and worries, apparently rather more deep than his, about the reality of the Communist threat.

This wisdom will express itself and be nourished only if we give it force and direction by our moral guidance, whatever our differences of opinion on tactic or timing, which in turn must result in the development and education of a will for peace among all our people. Together with the failure to provide a theology of peace, we must face the scandal of our failure to create a genuine will for peace. A positive, dedicated, dynamic will for peace, however, is not at all the same as an aversion for war. Sometimes I fear that all we have to work with on the level of emotions and the will is an almost exclusively physical aversion for war that hardly amounts to more than distaste for seeing blood (particularly one's own) all over the place or a reluctance to inflict (or endure) the grosser forms of physical pain. I must confess that I have detected a bit of this kind of queasiness in some of the things said in our own meetings.

Should aversion to war help to deepen our love for peace, fine. But by itself it contributes nothing to the building of that climate we of the church and synagogue owe, on the organic level, to those who are desperately struggling, despite their mistakes and their folly, toward world peace. A mere aversion to war often reveals itself only in the acute crises that threaten us from time to time; when the crises pass, we do not have attendance at parleys like this. Our job is to help build the love for peace that must motivate and sustain the work of religious moral education, beginning with ourselves, as well as the work of social justice, beginning with the other fellow. At the same time, we have the task of remaining faithful to the imperatives of moral wisdom.

It has become fashionable to dismiss airily, as devoid of significant content in our times, some of the neat distinctions of the traditional philosophies. Those of us who set store by them, however, never supposed that they constituted the sum of wisdom or contained the total treasure of truth. We saw them as convenient pegs on which to hang propositions, arguments, and points of view in order that these might be drained of their mere water and tested for their ultimate significance and worth.

One important distinction of the old scholastics may be applied with regard to the question of the will for peace: that between *velleitas* and *voluntas*. Although there is a widespread and tepid *velleitas* for peace, there is less evidence of a sustained, passionate *voluntas*. I seriously question the depth, the sincerity, and therefore the worth of such interest in peace as often exists among us. I suspect it is mere *velleitas* and short on effective *voluntas*. Indeed, *velleitas* is to *voluntas* as wishful thinking is to solid thought, as flirtation is to love. *Velleitas* is what moved the youthful Augustine, admiring from afar the beauty of chastity, to pray, "Lord make me chaste, but not too soon"; it is regard for a virtue we have no real intention or plan of mastering; it is a desire qualified by all manner of ifs, ands, and buts which one has no serious disposition to eliminate. *Voluntas*, on the other hand, is a fixed, stable, unqualified, total commitment. It may fail, but not by my fault, certainly not by my lack of desire, intention, and effort to win. It is to the *voluntas*, the efficacious will for peace, that we must unqualifiedly bind ourselves together. Granted there are areas in which we shall individually and in our separate groups continue to watch like hawks, however open to guilt by association with doves some of us on occasion may be. In studying, for example, the reports that come out of this parley and its workshops, some of us will by tradition be watching vigilantly lest there be any transgression of the lines of separation between church and state. I gather that Rabbi Weinstein had such a concern in mind when, in his keynote address, he valiantly suggested that missionary work be left to accredited missionaries! Others of us (I am definitely one) will be on guard against a kind of silent genocide operating in alleged service of peace, a by-product of some experiments in birth control imposed, however blandly or obliquely, as an instrument of national or international policy. Still others will be on guard against built-in temptations to neglect battles at home (domestic education programs or needed health and housing projects) under the alleged necessity of military programs abroad. But this parley will, please God, signalize our shared determination to talk even these things over, in accordance with our shared, overriding, unbreakable *voluntas* or will for peace.

As this is our main business in this parley, I am honor bound to speak for those who wish we had devoted more attention to the way in which organized religious groups can offer more positive support of the U.N. and its basic concepts in the years that lie ahead. There is widespread talk of the need for the revision of the U.N. Charter; a future symposium, bringing together international representatives of religion, might well face this question that the U.N. might more fully describe the tribute paid it by Pope Paul VI when he said: "The reason for this wish, which might be said to pertain to the structure of your Organization, leads us to complete it with other formulas. They are these: let no one, as a member of your Association, be superior to the others: not one above another. This is the formula of equality. We well know that there are other factors to be considered besides that of mere membership of this body. But equality, too, is a part of its constitution; not that you are equal, but that here you make yourselves equal. And it may be that for several among you this is an act of high

virtue; allow us to say this to you, we who represent a religion
which works salvation through the humility of its divine Founder.
It is impossible to be a brother, if one is not humble. For it is pride,
however inevitable it may seem, which provides tensions, struggles
for prestige, predominance, colonialism, selfishness; it is pride that
shatters brotherhood."

Some European newspapers that carried this message won-
dered what the American reaction would be. The Irish paper
Hibernia, for example, editorially asked: "Will the Pope's visit to
the United Nations have any lasting results?" Their question is per-
tinent to us. Will our parley have any lasting results? The same
spirit that motivated Pope Paul VI motivated those who called this
parley, those of every religious tradition.

There is no doubt that there was immediate approval of both
the Pope's message and his visit. Indeed, the favorable response
indicates the extent of the desire for peace that exists in human
hearts everywhere. But the sorry truth is that the plea of His Holi-
ness for nations to discard the weapons of war and to devote the
consequent savings to helping the poor, the sick, and the disinher-
ited is unlikely to persuade secretaries of defense to scrap a single
rifle, tank, plane, or nuclear bomb from their vast arsenals. The
United States will not. Neither will the Soviet Union, although its
representatives also joined heartily in the general applause.

Quite as unlikely, one fears, is the probability that the "great
powers" (ourselves included) will welcome the status of "equals"
with the small nations, all the rhetoric about "equality before the
law" to the contrary. And so *Hibernia's* most pointed question calls
for honest answers. What effective steps can be taken to guarantee
equality of voice to "great powers" and "little people" alike? The
United States will not enjoy receiving a mandate from small Asian
and African nations enjoining it from undertaking Latin American
interventions. The Soviet Union will not be happy at being ordered
by small nations to take down the Berlin Wall. But *Hibernia* sees
no other possible road to peace, and they suspect that the Pope
sees no other practical course either.

What do we, in this parley, think? All we know is that, if we
are to second the efforts of the Pope (and on this point no one here
will dissent, since in fact he was seconding the efforts of those
everywhere who love peace), we must extend the range of our

dialogue and therefore our moral influence toward the creation of an international outlook that sets equality among peoples in its moral context. Hence, if our first objective was *aggiornamento* in the sense of taking stock of our own behavior, balancing our own books, and sifting our own moral teachings to find our areas of agreement, our second is to work toward the creation of an urgently needed wider symposium, that representatives of religious groups in other nations may discover ways of agreement on the moral principles that are increasingly clear to us.

The spiritual teachers of the world are obliged to preach to heads of state the duties of their respective vocations, the dreadful responsibilities that are theirs, and the eternal sanctions that surround their temporal decisions. But they must also be the first to recognize that these decisions do lie, once the moral imperatives have been proclaimed, with the temporal authorities and that they, the heads of state, have a moral claim on our support in their effort to do the job that is theirs so long as they do not so violate the mandates of morality as to become destructive of the purposes for which they hold their posts.

Our constant prayer should be one as sincere as our occasional witness of protest, that the heads of states will so discharge their duties as to be called with right the peacemakers who are the children of God. Our further prayer is that we ourselves shall not be found wanting in providing the moral climate in which they can effectively do so.

9

The Limitations and
Possibilities for Peace

*The Executive Committee of the conference wanted to have jour-
nalists who knew the workings and ways of organized religion to
judge its actions in the field of peace. Accordingly a luncheon was
reserved for this purpose and three leading religious journalists
were invited to speak on a uniform topic, "The Limitations and
Possibilities of Organized Religion Acting for Peace." The three
papers follow.*

MSGR. SALVATORE ADAMO

The ways of peace are manifold. They embrace such contraries
as total pacifism and limited war. Yes, even war can be a pathway
to peace. The recently concluded Vatican Council proclaimed:
"Those who devote themselves to military service should regard
themselves as the agents of security and freedom. . . They are making a genuine contribution to the establishment of peace." For
warriors impose justice on the nations and justice is the mother of
peace.

Admittedly, the ways of peace can be perverted. War may
become a means of brutal conquest with tyranny, not equity, its
outcome, while total pacifism may lead to craven submission to

the darksome equity of universal terror. Like nuclear power, potential instruments of peace can be used to build up a new world or destroy an old one. Governments and their people will decide which usage will prevail; religion offers light so that the right decision may be made.

Indeed, organized religion not only can but must guide the people and, through them, governments to employ the best available means to attain peace. This movement begins to take shape when religious persons become actively involved in peace movements. Toward this end the religious press has an important role to fill: to inform, to encourage, to support all those traveling the many roads to peace.

Our first move would seem to be the creation of the precondition of peace and the eradication of the precondition of war. Today the great precondition of war is an obsessive, pervasive fear of communism—particularly in America—as well as a corresponding fear of capitalism—particularly in mainland China. Both are not without internal political overtones. In America, our chief concern, it has led to a policy of containment and brinkmanship in Berlin, Cuba, and Vietnam. Apart from the merits or demerits of such diplomacy, it contravenes the Christian concept of the brotherhood of man. The idea that man constitutes a human family originated by God must give rise to mutual trust and co-operation among nations, must dispel the poisonous atmosphere of fear. Surely if we wish to have peace, we must begin by settling the cold war.

Was not that the goal Pope Paul VI set for the U.N. when he told the General Assembly last October: "You work here not only to avert conflicts between states, but also to make them capable of working for each other. You are not satisfied with facilitating mere coexistence between nations; you take a much greater step forward, one deserving of our praise and our support: you organize the brotherly collaboration of peoples."

Toward this end the religious press, recognizing the solidarity of mankind, must urge the inclusion of all nations in the U.N. This means that mainland China should be invited to join. The cold war, that frigid fountainhead of so many conflicts and near-conflicts since the end of World War II, can never be resolved so long as three fourths of a billion people are outside the pale of the

U.N. Therefore, we should promote mainland China's admission to the U.N. without prejudicing Formosa's right also to be there.

Likewise a hand of friendship must be extended to Cuba as it has been to Yugoslavia and even Soviet Russia itself. One may ask, how can there be friendliness with those who hate us, those who claim they will bury us? How can we ever be at peace with regimes that derive their dynamism from dialectical materialism, that look upon conflict as the natural and ineluctable fate of man? It was Pope John XXIII who in his world letter, *Peace on Earth*, reminded us "to make a clear distinction between a false philosophy of the natural origin and purpose of men and the world, and the economic, social, cultural, and political undertakings, even when such undertakings draw their origin and inspiration from that philosophy." . . . It may sometimes happen, therefore, that meetings arranged for some practical end—though hitherto they were thought to be altogether useless—may in fact be fruitful at the present time, or at least offer prospects of success.

The religious press as the voice of organized religion commenting on current history must seek to galvanize all men of good will to speak to one another and behave like brothers. Lest anyone imagine that such a proposal is hopelessly naive, let me recall Norman Cousins' article in the *Saturday Review* last year in which he described the beneficial impact of Pope John's friendliness to Soviet Russia. During his interview with Khrushchev, Cousins reported: "The matter came up of the Pope's moral intervention during the week of the Cuban missile crisis. Mr. Khrushchev said at that time that the Pope's appeal for restraint had had considerable weight in his thinking. In fact, he said it was the first ray of light in the fast-developing darkness."

Mr. Cousins added: "When I reported to Pope John on the mission to Moscow, I found him most pleased by Khrushchev's response to his call upon world leaders for responsibility and restraint and for an end to nuclear terror. The Pope said he had deliberately avoided polemics against the Soviet Union in recent years because of his belief that meaningful and useful communication would at some time be critically essential. Besides, he added, it was much too late for denunciations; there was time only to try to prevent an unspeakable holocaust."

Yes, we must strive to terminate the cold war, lest it become transformed into monstrous nuclear war. For unbridled nuclear war must be resisted at all costs by all sane and saintly people. As the Vatican Council put it: "Any act of war aimed indiscriminately at the destruction of entire cities or extensive areas along with their population is a crime against God and man himself. It merits unequivocal and unhesitating condemnation." We must press for nuclear disarmament and then general disarmament. Perhaps a first step in this direction would be to ask each nuclear power to make a solemn pledge not to be the first to use nuclear bombs anywhere.

In pursuing these various pathways to peace, we cannot afford to ignore the soldier, whose role is not only that of defender but also of peacemaker. Now the soldier is indeed the national policeman, serving to solve disputes between nations peacefully, resorting to force of arms only in the interest of justice. Someday the soldier may be the international police of an international government that will more effectively impose justice on disputing nations and so end national wars, just as national sovereignties today preclude lesser wars between their sub-states. In line with this idea, we may remember Cardinal Ottaviani's summons to the Council Fathers to issue an appeal to the nations to form a world republic in which even ideological war would be banned. No religious leader ever made more daring, forward-looking proposals. Nor are they visionary ideals but postulates for survival in a nuclear age. In the name of human brotherhood, they must be advocated and advanced.

Finally, the religious press must give a voice to the peace-prophet, the total pacifist. His refusal to bear arms in any cause must be acknowledged as meaningful for society. As he is ready to surrender all earthly goods, even his own life, rather than inflict death on any man, ought not the rest of the community make sure its cause is just and all avenues of reconciliation have been exhausted before it resorts to violence?

However, the peace-prophet, or the conscientious objector, has no more right to expect the community to accept his way as the only way to peace, than the nun to expect all people to embrace virginity or the monk to desire all men to accept poverty. Their ways promote a spirit of chastity and detachment among people. If they, however, should ever mistake their role and imagine their special vocations are to be accepted by all men, they will only discredit their good example by overstating its feasibility. They must not permit the best to make war against the good. The peace-prophet must evaluate his position realistically, lest he end up as "a voice crying in the wilderness."

In order to be effectively heard, every peacemaker, no matter what road he chooses, must strive to make his position as reasonable and feasible as possible, so that a consensus for a vast peace-movement may be reached. Even so, however, the struggle for peace will be but half-won. After all, it takes two to wage war and it takes two to wage peace. There is, unfortunately, no unilateral pathway to peace.

ARTHUR MOORE

Do organized religions have the right to consider problems of war and peace? The answer, of course, is yes. This may seem to some a mere cliché, but given the extremely wide spectrum of contemporary opinion about what religion should or should not do, it is useful to emphasize this point.

To those of us who get letters from readers or telephone calls from parishioners, it may not seem immediately evident that this point is generally acknowledged. It is nevertheless true. No matter how angry the reaction may be to any given statement, the basic attack, ultimately, is almost always on the content of the statement rather than upon the right of the religious group to make a statement of some kind about war and peace.

Within Protestantism, there are two loose groupings that might seem exceptions to this rule. On the one hand, there are those (usually fundamentalist) whose conception of religion is so personal that the idea of the church in any sense except as a number of individuals is really non-existent. Historically, this seems to be a rather unstable condition, for when time gathers them into groups they begin to make statements just like the rest of us (although perhaps a bit more cautiously at first).

At the other end of the spectrum are those people whose theological commitment to the vocation of the Christian in the secular world would seem to minimize the usefulness of religious groups as such making pronouncements. This is more a theoretical than a practical problem, however, for in real life these people show a passionate devotion to issuing statements on every conceivable subject.

Generally, then, the question of peace is one that has historically always been within the church's domain and is a subject on which it is not only permitted, but is indeed expected, to speak.

From this truth we must turn to another self-evident fact— one that few would even trouble to deny—which is that the vast majority of the statements made by religious groups about war and peace have no effect whatsoever except to make the drafters feel good. They do not seriously influence anybody, either within or outside the churches. It is not so much that they are received with scorn as that they make no impression. All too quickly people tend to forget that they were issued, let alone remember their content. They are, in short, a waste of time. This is somewhat overstated and there are obvious exceptions. But there is enough truth in this sweeping generalization to make it worth while to examine some of the causes of our failure in this field.

There is, first, the fact that we have only one basic thing to say. We are for peace; we are against war. Who is not? In an age when even generals talk like pacifists, there is no one except possibly the late Adolf Hitler who can be expected to come out foursquare for war. Thus, to be against war is like being against sin; and to leave such a statement at this general level is merely to avoid the issues.

Unfortunately, when we descend from this broad level to specific issues, we find that we are much divided among ourselves. To take the most obvious example, pacifists and non-pacifists have very different assumptions about the nature and use of power. Can, then, a group in which both are involved put out a statement to which all can subscribe, or must there be separate statements? The usual solution is to put out a statement which papers over the differences—a statement which can in effect be read in different ways by different groups. The problem with this approach, however, is that it sacrifices a point of view for consensus. A statement which can be read in several different ways probably cannot be read with much conviction in any way.

On a lower level, many of the difficulties arise from the abominable practice of having statements written by committees. Anything written by a committee can be read only by a committee.

To speak of consensus is to bring up still another problem. Consensus as it is usually understood refers to those who draft the statement. A consensus of the total membership among a religious group is frequently assumed and very seldom sought. I do not wish to espouse any kind of lowest-common-denominator agreement, but how often is there general debate throughout an organization before a position is taken which often claims to speak for that group? Those people in leadership in churches have often left themselves open to the charge of having spoken *for* their membership without having spoken *to* them. There are, of course, reasons for this—timing, problems of communication, etc.—but it does tend to give the average church member a feeling that the position taken is one in which he is uninvolved and for which he has no responsibility.

All of which brings us to the thorny problem of authority. What kind of authority do pronouncements by religious groups have? I have already suggested that in practical effect they have next to none. But what kind are they supposed to have? The problem of all religious activity is that we long to hear the voice of God and all too often we hear only the tones of pompous old Joe and stupid old Bill. This discrepancy has grave consequences in the area of war and peace, for it affects the whole question of tone.

What religion is traditionally supposed to do about wars is to enact a ritualistic role. It may say, "War is bad, but this war is okay. You have done a wicked thing, but you are forgiven." Now, I don't mean to make cheap fun of the absolving function, for, clearly, its purpose is to be reassuring. But the authority of such a position is distilled from the experience and needs of the community.

The other religious function—commonly called the prophetic —is to attack the community's position in the name of a superior moral insight. This is the role that we would all lay claim to, but the prophet business is not so easy as it may seem. It requires a constant self-examination as rigorous as the examination we give to others. This is painful, equally painful to liberals and conservatives.

Too, the successful prophet should work himself out of a job. There is nothing so stale as being prophetic about a situation that has already been taken care of. Yet nature is such that we tend to refer to the known, and deal with a current crisis in terms of the last crisis.

It is, in short, not always easy to locate and define the exact nature of the moral issue in a conflict. Far too often we substitute a statement reiterating our previous wisdom rather than going through the agonizing process of debate, discussion, and self-searching that is necessary for a fresh appraisal of a new set of circumstances. This may be fine as an anxiety-relieving device, but it tends to deaden the moral climate.

The role of a prophet is not an easy one and the role of an institutional prophet may be an impossible one. It is usually the institutions, and most notably the churches, against whom the prophets are being prophetic. Expecting our large, cumbersome organized religious groups to be prophetic is rather like asking a computer to sing a love song.

What can we do to help increase the chances of this unlikely occurrence? Paradoxically, we might begin by abandoning the comfortable notion that religious groups have a right to speak, and say instead that they have an obligation to speak on this subject, but that, if they are to be really listened to, they must *earn* the right.

Obviously this means that those of us who are involved must do our homework and learn how governments arrive at policy decisions. This is an elementary approach, of course, but one which is nevertheless indispensable, for we still tend to retreat to moral generalities when the going gets tough. If I were the Secretary of State or the Secretary of Defense and a church group came to tell me that war was bad, I expect that I would also assume the blank, disengaged look that has been observed on the faces of government officials listening to church groups. Unfortunately, statesmen do not assume that look often enough and they are apt to soak up our spongy moralisms and give them right back to us.

On the other hand, we have only one Secretary of State and we should not pretend that we occupy that position. Eugene Carson Blake has observed that much of what the church has had to say about foreign policy has "sounded like analyses of foreign policy by third-echelon State Department people who are not responsible for actual policy." Paul Ramsey has a valid point in questioning the qualifications of many clergymen to speak on specific points of foreign policy (although he tends to make rather too much of this point).

If we are not exhorters or actual makers of policy, what is our function as members of an organized religion? Let me quote again from Dr. Blake. This passage was not written about war and peace but about the pastorate in general.

> Too many pastors have failed to find any real theological connection between what is expected of them as preacher, pastor and leader of a community of worship, on the one hand, and as a leader of relevant ethical and social change on the other side ... Those who have lost an appreciation of what a worshiping community may be become frustrated social workers or politicians. And those who give up on the radical ethical drive of the Gospel break down under the pressures and irrelevancies of trying to be a professional chaplain to an essentially secular people.*

Our job is to find the connection between the great ethical insights that we proclaim and the events, ominous and confusing, taking place in the world today. Such a task is hard and frustrating. It was André Gide who warned, "Do not understand me too quickly." And so it is with God's purposes in this world. We must keep seeking and striving for the connections, aware that the connections we find may not be the ones God intended us to find. A realization of this should lead us to humility. We must begin to realize that it is not our role to give the world answers that we already possess but to join with the world in searching for the answers. For every new problem there is a new answer.

We might well begin at home. I do not think that most churches engage in enough internal dialogue. But internal dialogue must never cause us to abandon our dialogue with the rest of the world, for it is there that we must, in the words of T.S. Eliot, "work out our salvation with diligence."

RABBI STEVEN S. SCHWARZSCHILD

The job of "religion" is primarily to serve God without reservations. Now, if God commands us to serve our fellow men, as

* "The Church in the Next Decade," *Christianity and Crisis*, Vol. XXVI, No. 2 (February 21, 1966), pp. 15–18.

indeed He does, then this is our secondary obligation—dependent on our primary obligation to God. This hierarchical ordering of our religious obligations is neither intended to be nor in fact results in a relative derogation of our social duties; to the very contrary—and this is my point—it makes our social duties the more radically imperative. If our social obligations were primary, then they would all be qualified by one another as well as by other considerations: peace would have to be correlated with patriotism, justice with love, truth with respect, etc. As it is, however, these and other human tasks devolve upon us with an absolute, unqualified demand for obedience: God Himself imposes them upon us.

God, now, is radical. He is the most radical of all radicals. (I am not using a titillating neologism, but translate a classic scholastic idiom that speaks of Him as *'ikkar ha'ikkarim*—"the root of all roots." As Karl Marx reminds us in a famous passage, to be radical means to go to the root. Marx went on to claim that the root of man is man. We hold that the root of man is God.)

Therefore, when God, the Radical, demands that we seek peace, He demands radically that we radically seek radical peace. If I may paraphrase what Justice Black once said about the First Amendment to the Constitution, we are naive enough to think that when God said "Seek peace and pursue it!" (Psalm 34:14), He did not mean "seek war," nor did He mean "seek peace when it is prudent, popular, or conducive to your interests"—nor yet did He mean "seek peace slowly, under certain and not under other conditions." Because the God of the religious man is the root of all radicalism, the religious man himself is bound to be radical in every respect, including in his insistence on peace. In specific terms, it is clear that, even as the civil-rights movement demands justice—all of it, here and now, and in all ways—so the peace movement demands peace—only peace, immediately, everywhere —in the methods of operation as well as with respect to the goal.

This is neither the time nor the place to enter into detailed theological or political debates. However, before I go on to deduce some conclusions from the propositions we have thus far enunciated, in order not to be misunderstood as a naive utopian and sentimental idealist (the usual phrases thrown into the considerations at this point), I must state that we are perfectly aware of the scriptural, canon-legal, theological, and even political difficulties that ensue upon such statements. Let me merely say that we do not believe that by making such radical pacifistic demands do we in the least mistake ourselves as self-redeeming sinless persons; we merely demand of ourselves radical obedience to God, so that He may, in His time and way, bring about His Kingdom. We also do not realistically expect ourselves or society to be capable of immediately and completely obeying the Divine command to peacefulness. I am merely saying that "religion" is in the business of, uncompromisingly and radically, demanding the full understanding of and obedience to God's call—and we are profoundly and painfully aware of the difference between hearing and making a demand, on the one hand, and, on the other, fulfilling it.

The insistence on religion's radicalism is important for two reasons, one appertaining to religion itself, the other to its effectiveness in today's society. So far as the former is concerned, for all too long, first in practice and then also in theory, it has been theological fashion to speak of the need for religion's relevancy and realism. A distinction was made between the perfect law of God and the prudently proximate applications of this law in history. This distinction led to a number of results—the belief that we were under the Divine obligation to obey God's law only insofar as possible, that we could properly judge—and beforehand, at that— what the limits of the possible were at any given time, and that religion itself was to make these compromises. As if there were not always enough politicians, journalists, popularizers, and other assorted realists around to make these compromises for us. The fact is that, on the ethical spectrum, religion defines—or should define— the Left, paganism defines the Right, the politicians define the consensus of the center; and the further to the Right religion places itself, the further yet to the Right will the politicians settle their moral compromises. The social role of authentic faith is not to be acceptable to society, but to pull it in the right direction.

I come now to the practical social effect of the betrayal of the radicalism of religion. It is by now a cliché that American religion came to the civil-rights struggle very belatedly. The militant pioneers of the civil-rights movement, when they saw us arriving in Selma, were too polite at first to articulate audibly: "Where have you been all these years?" (I will not even discuss the propriety of the clergy then pushing themselves, or letting themselves be pushed, into the front-center of the press pictures of the march.) Organized religion has, at best, been the tail on the kite of the civil-rights movement. For certain limited practical, political purposes, this may be of value, but for purposes of ethical and social, not to speak of religious, advance, this posture is completely useless. The civil rightniks knew that they had got where they were without religion; if religion now wanted to join them, that might be all right; but it remained clear to them that, wherever they wanted to go from here, they would again have to go without religion—religion might or might not follow.

Obviously, neither civil rights nor religion has been usefully served by this history. Had religion, on the other hand, been as radical about civil rights as surely its own inner nature should compel it to be—had it asked for complete equality at least fifty years ago, then and there and all of it, not a little here and a little there (see Isaiah 28) and small doses as the power structure permitted—we would have been in Selma before SNCC, SNCC might feel a little different about religion, and America today might look considerably different.

And now the demands for peace are being raised. Let us face the facts. Peacefulness in word and deed, individually and socially, has been the theme for quite a long time in certain sections of the academic community, in some portions of the intelligentsia, above all in the vague complex called the peace movement—the overwhelmingly larger portions of which have no relationship whatsoever to "organized religion." The teach-in movement was completely secular. If it were not for these small struggling groups and for the few individuals who courageously raised their voices over the last three years, the conscience of the U.S. Senate, but for Senators Morse and Gruening, would have died completely so far as peace in Vietnam is concerned. To use a Chassidic metaphor, these men put the cold compresses on the aching head of the United States to keep it alive until the doctor arrived—if he ever will. At this point, once again to get around to proclaiming one's "concern," to want to raise polite questions when what is urgently needed is a courageous and useful stand of opposition, to fawn on the Establishment by constantly pounding on President Johnson's proven desire for peace, and to demand a compromise on the battlefield as well as at the negotiating table, is all over again to make oneself irrelevant.

The fact is that the demand for theological realism has led to total irrelevance. And the much maligned utopian idealists— more commonly found in the scruffy offices of student organizations than in the comfortable pews—have turned out to have more of an effect on America and the world than careful, respectable religious leaders and organizations. If God is radical, to be radical is to be Godly; if God is everlastingly relevant, then to be relevant is to be Godly. And now let us ask where religion is to be found— on the campus or in the church or synagogue? I suggest that the relationship between religion and peace is that, not only when it fits into the political plans of our government, nor only when it is socially safe to talk about it, nor yet to the degree to which this seems practically prudent and promising of results, but under the irresistible command of God, always, everywhere, in every way, and totally, religion must insist on, explore, and practice the ways of peace toward the attainment of peace.

Again, by way of protecting my theological and ethical flanks, I assert the theoretical validity and the practical realism of this view of the matter. Absolute insistence on peace does not mean that we do not, of course, fully realize that there are moral and social values other than peace, and that one or the other of them may even be superior to peace itself; we are only saying that no other human values can, especially in our historical epoch, be conceivably attained outside of a relatively peaceful society. And in terms of political realism, unless religion proposes and enacts a peace program in accord with its own Divine radicalism far ahead of the pragmatic peace programs of governments, social scientists, and independent social movements, religion will again rightly be regarded as the moralistic straggler behind the real world that advances either into greater human dignity or into self-destruction.

I turn, finally and briefly, to the role of the religious press in this drama. Here I sit in a glass house, because, as far as I can remember, my own journal has published during the four years that I have been its editor only one substantial theological treatment of questions of peace and war, and that was a translation of a Hebrew pamphlet written in Russia during the first world war.

This itself may, however, be a symptom of our problem. At least in Jewish circles, even when the Ichud circle at the University of Jerusalem is taken into account, an incredibly small amount of attention is being paid to this complex of problems by knowledgeable and qualified thinkers and leaders. (This parallels our national comparative expenditures on the preparations for war and peace.) What one usually sees are at best preachy exhortations mixed of recent *New York Times* editorials and vague apostrophes to pacific virtues. Isaiah 2 is regarded as an indefinitely postponed dream rather than as an immediate messianic action program. Two urgent desiderata emerge, then, from this situation for the religious press: hard-headed, literate thinking must be stimulated which takes Micah 4 more seriously than Dean Acheson's or Hans Morgenthau's latest ideologizing; and the courage to risk the favor of the conventional reading public. Whether we are relevant to the religious bourgeoisie and the power structure is considerably less important than whether we are relevant to the pioneering social and intellectual forces operative in our society today.

Specifically, I would make two proposals. The first is that, in discussions and written interchanges between politicians and religions, the working papers—in terms of which the ensuing analyses unavoidably have to take place—be prepared by religious thinkers rather than by the politicians. Let the politicians tackle the problems of the world in terms of a radical theology of ethics and society, rather than religion always having to come along and take ineffectual glancing pot-shots at the over-all plans and surveys of the political scientists. In plain English, the vocabulary, the system of concepts and of values ought to derive from the Bible and religion rather than from the Rand Corporation and the Harvard or Columbia schools of Russian studies. Here, too, the superstitious awe of the so-called experts, of which even President Kennedy got his fill at the Bay of Pigs, has prevailed far too long.

My second proposal is that the religious press begin to think about filling a lacuna that even the best of the general press has conspicuously left open. The world newspaper of record is *The New York Times; The Times* prints at inordinate length all the statements issued by government agencies for the record, i.e., for propaganda. The real working papers in government agencies almost never see the light of public scrutiny. There can surely be little doubt that the American people and the people of the world would shrink back in horror if they ever got a glimpse at the realistic plans that circulate in inner government offices about pre-emptive war, secret foreign machinations, and preparations for domestic losses when Armageddon comes. To bring this about would serve the ideals of peace, democracy, freedom of the press, and the preservation of mankind. Cannot the religious press be expected to do something toward that end?

We began by reminding ourselves that God is "the root of all radicals." This is, if not understood, at least proclaimed by all religionists. We all hold, furthermore, that the one supreme task of religion is to "spread the name of God throughout the world." The syllogism is completed when we remind ourselves, finally, that, not as a modern fashion, but at the very heart of Biblical religion, the name of God which we are called upon to glorify is Peace: "Rabbi Yudan ben Rabbi Jose said: 'Great is peace, for God's name is Peace, as it is said.'" (Judges 6:24) "And Gideon called it The Lord Peace—so it is to this day." (Lev. R., Tsav, IX:9)

The Evolution of a Position Paper

Three position papers were commissioned by the conference, written by experts in advance, and distributed to participants in advance. Those written for the first two workshops were modified only slightly into their reports, while that written for the third workshop—"Forms of Intervention: Moral Responsibilities and Limits"—was modified greatly by members of the workshop with the help of the three discussants.

The evolution of this position paper into the final report was a dynamic process. Each workshop met for a total of eleven hours. This time span was not sufficient for this third workshop and it held its last meeting from 11 p.m. to approximately 2 a.m. in order to reach substantial if not unanimous agreement. Some of its recommendations were further modified on the floor of the plenary.

In order to indicate something of the process of reaching the final report, the text of the position paper is given below, as is the abbreviated texts of initial commentaries by the three discussants.

1. *The Original Paper*

FORMS OF INTERVENTION:
MORAL RESPONSIBILITIES AND LIMITS *

The religious faiths and institutions of the West have a special role to play in examining the premises of "intervention" by one or another government in the affairs of another country. Their special role arises from the way in which the religious institutions and their religious messages have been used as the ultimate justifications for intervention. For the modern military actions of the great powers do not always rest on economic, directly military-strategic, or even national-interest *realpolitisch* reasons, and certainly actions rarely can be justified in those terms. They demand reasons more "religious" in tone, more grandly ideological in spirit: to "protect the free world," to "oppose atheistic communism," to "turn back the forces of tyranny," or, alternatively, to "protect the socialist camp," to "oppose anti-humanist capitalism," to "turn back the forces of imperialism." In short, the values that have long been proclaimed by our varied religious institutions are now advanced to justify the use of "legitimate" violence by the state.

When the state did this on behalf of one faith, we called it an Establishment of religion; now that the state claims to do it on behalf of all the faiths jointly, we must recognize the practice as only another, more subtle, and—in the modern world—perhaps more dangerous Establishment. As men of God and men of liberty both, we in the United States have always opposed the Establishment of religion; now, aware of the new forms taken by a more dangerous crusade, we have the special responsibility to say that *we* will advance our values and our visions, by using *our* means of spiritual appeal; that we do not need and do not want the state to try to advance our values at the point of a gun or the drop of a bomb. For just as it was not the truth of Judaism or of Roman-Hellenistic philosophy that was advanced when Jesus was executed, nor the truth of Christianity that was advanced when the Crusaders slaughtered Moslems and Jews, so it is not the truth of either Judaism or Christianity, or the great Western values that spring from

* Drafted by Dr. Jacob B. Agus, Mr. Tilford Dudley, and Dr. Arthur I. Waskow.

them, that is advanced when American planes bomb Buddhists or Communists in Vietnam. Nor was it the truth of communism that was advanced when Russian tanks smashed Budapest; for it is not only the Western states that have conscripted "religion," ideology, and moral values to the service of the state, as fig leaves for military intervention.

It is on these grounds that we claim the right, and the responsibility, to speak in judgment on the forms of intervention used by various governments throughout the world in dealing with countries weaker than their own.

As to what forms of intervention may be legitimate for the United States (or for any other nation), two basic moral principles must be kept in mind. The first is that no human institution is or can be perfect in moral virtue; that therefore power, unchecked, does evil in the world; that therefore no government may be allowed to judge in its own case or to see itself as the redeemer of mankind, the perfect bearer of perfect justice. The second is that the means used in any act must, to be moral, stand in close relation to the ends sought; that the noblest ends do not, by their mere statement, justify the use of any means; that the legitimacy of means must be assessed according to their actual effects and not by the rhetoric that unleashed them.

We are used to applying these standards to the actions of governments other than our own, particularly to those totalitarian governments that we see as claiming to be redeemers of mankind and as using means utterly incommensurate with that claim, though "justified" by it. We are not so used to applying these standards to our own government; but we must now insist that these standards be applied in any assessment of American foreign policy that claims to be based on the view that our god is God, and not government.

To these most basic moral principles we add one important moral-political judgment: that in world politics, as in all human politics, there is power in moral ideas and values, that to the question, "How many divisions has the Pope?" must be given the answer, "At the heart of every division lie the churches of the world." Thus, not only in discussing the issue of intervention in the abstract, but in deciding for or against particular interventions, institutions of moral judgment—universities, churches, voluntary organizations, movements of moral and political renovation—must play a direct and major role.

From these precepts we have drawn three major conclusions. First, from the principle of avoiding the imputation of absolute virtue to any government, we conclude that certain forms of intervention must be reviewed and authorized by mankind generally. Second, from the principle of the interconnection of means and ends, we conclude that the particular means used by the United States must be carefully analyzed, and changes made. Finally, from the principle of the power of moral values, we conclude that the churches of the world must themselves organize new institutions for the better bringing to bear of moral power. We propose, in the three sections following, to examine each of these conclusions in detail.

1 - *The Control of Military Intervention by Mankind*

In regard to the problem of controlling, through a system of checks and balances, the propensity of any one government to intervene in the affairs of another country, we should keep in mind that intervention of whatever kind is most likely to occur in one of two situations: when in some country there is domestic civil war and the economic, political, ideological, or other interests of one or more of the great powers are threatened (as in the Congo, the Dominican Republic, Hungary, Vietnam); and when the building or strengthening of a military alliance seems suddenly intensely threatening to one of the powers against which the alliance is intended to guard (as in the Cuban missile crisis, the Berlin crisis, the Quemoy-Matsu crisis). Different techniques may be required for dealing with these two rather different kinds of situations; in particular, it may be possible to change the way in which nations deal with intervention in domestic civil wars more quickly than the way in which they intervene to protect themselves against what seem like military threats.

To examine the ways in which checks and balances might be applied to the decisions of governments to intervene, the use of political and economic power in what might be called "co-operative intervention" must first be distinguished from the use of military coercion. There can be no doubt that economic aid, trade, information broadcasts, cultural exchanges, etc., are all forms of "intervention" by one government or society in the lives of another. But, they are the kinds of intervention that (until there is a world government and probably even then) national governments must by their nature use, so long as they are political and economic instruments that dispose of a "foreign" policy and make judgments about tariffs, investments, public speeches, etc. Moreover, they are by nature co-operative, not coercive. Radio broadcasts are effective in presenting a new and unorthodox view of the world only if they attract listeners and win agreement; economic or educational aid can change a country only in ways the country finds suitable. (Indeed, these forms of intervention are so essentially co-operative that they might well be developed into a two-way street: Kenyan peace-corpsmen in the United States, as well as U.S. peace-corpsmen in Kenya.) The use of military power upon other nations, on the other hand, is not "co-operative": it is directly coercive, and can be used to impose, rather than urge or encourage, change. Nor is military action an inherent result of simply being a national government—as some states, like Switzerland and Sweden, have proved during long histories. Although some forms of economic and political power can be used to coerce—boycotts and embargoes, for instance—military power is peculiarly immediate in its coercive effect, peculiarly brutal, and therefore peculiarly dangerous. It most needs to be regulated by the checks and balances dictated by a religious or political realism.

To look especially at the recent history of U.S. military intervention in the affairs of other countries—intervention that should especially interest and concern us as Americans hopeful that liberty and justice be protected and expanded in the world—we find it most dubious that military intervention has served these purposes, and we believe it would have been most useful to have had proposals for these interventions subjected to the judgment of others before they were carried out.

In Greece, the military intervention of the United States on one side of a civil war followed the military intervention of several Communist states on the other side. The better solution would

have been international action to prevent military intervention—
the provision of arms or armed men—on either side. As it happened, the American intervention did not end the civil war until
the provision of arms from the other side was ended by the de-
fection of Yugoslavia from its Soviet alliance. And the continued
provision of military aid to Greece strengthened an army that has
been regarded by many Greeks as antagonistic to democratic
decision-making within the country and that has, during the past
year, been the major bone of contention in political disorder within
Greece.

In the Dominican Republic, the military intervention of the
United States on one side of an incipient civil war has (on the testimony of Senator J. William Fulbright, *The New York Times,*
Theodore Draper, and other qualified observers) thwarted a democratic social revolution; pinned the country to a precarious *status
quo* in which all social change, though badly needed, seems to
threaten some crucial interest and can therefore not be undertaken; undermined throughout the Western Hemisphere a slowly
and painfully built system of co-operation and independence; and
undermined throughout the world the legal and political restraints
against military intervention by other great powers in their smaller
neighbors or semidependents.

In Vietnam, the military intervention of the United States on
one side of a civil war has not slowed down (and indeed has probably speeded up) the military intervention of Communist governments on the other side; has not guaranteed the blessings of liberty
either to the Vietnamese today or to their posterity but instead has
strengthened an army and government that are not responsible to
democratic controls and that have frequently suppressed newspapers and repressed public dissent; and has involved the United
States in uncontrolled bombings and burnings of civilian villages
believed to be harboring the enemy, and in destruction of the
"enemy" rice crop in a way that only twenty years ago was considered by the U.S. Navy itself to be a violation of the laws of war.

In the case of the Cuban missile crisis, naval intervention by
the United States in fear of the consequences of a military alliance

between Cuba and the Soviet Union put the world in jeopardy of thermonuclear collision; cast doubt upon the international law of the open seas, with possible disastrous consequences in the future; placed the United States in the peculiar position (morally difficult to defend) of justifying its own intervention to prevent the establishment of missile bases near its territory while itself establishing similar missile bases near the territory of other great powers; accomplished only the minimal result of the withdrawal of the particular missiles challenged, while reducing not one whit the far greater danger to itself and to world peace of missiles in submarines off its shore and missiles poised to attack it from half a world away; and probably encouraged China to believe that since the Soviet atomic umbrella could not be depended on by Cuba or other Soviet allies, China and other underdeveloped countries should seek to produce their own nuclear weapons.

We are not suggesting that American military intervention in any of these cases was the sole, or the major, evil. We are saying that in every case a far better response to the situation would have been action by a wider international body that could have acted both to prevent or end any military intervention that had already taken place from anywhere else, and to prevent military intervention by the United States. And we are saying further, that if this structure applies to intervention carried on by the United States, it applies even more strongly to that carried on by the United Kingdom, France, the Soviet Union, China, and other powers during the last fifteen years.

What system of checks and balances could have controlled such military interventions as these? The only world-wide institution capable of success in this endeavor is the U.N. (Regional organizations are not only frequently dominated by one great power, as are the Organization of American States and the Warsaw Pact, but are also frequently extremely hostile to one or a few countries in the region—as is the Arab League. They do not, therefore, represent any reasonable check on the power of an individual state or a coalition to use its strength in dangerous and immoral ways.) We therefore propose that at once, so far as military intervention in domestic civil wars is concerned, and, within a decade,

so far as intervention in defense against a feared alliance is concerned, it be agreed that positive authorization by the U.N. is
necessary before any national government may carry on a military
intervention by the provision of military aid, by the stationing of
military forces, or by outright military attack.

In the case of intervention in domestic civil wars, we specifically mean that military intervention by any nation on behalf of
either side should be prohibited unless and until the U.N. has
authorized it. It cannot be held legitimate to intervene on behalf
of a constituted government but illegitimate to intervene on behalf
of a revolutionary movement. Indeed, any effort by the United
States to apply such a discriminatory rule would belie our own
revolutionary past and would betray those people who, groaning
under totalitarian governments or under exploitative social systems, want to overthrow their governments. On the other hand,
the Soviet and Chinese argument that military support for revolution is legitimate but for an established government is illegitimate
simply means that external action could sooner or later overturn,
or at least throw into unending turmoil, even the most popularly
based, most democratically responsible governments in the world.
If the rule we are proposing had been in effect, both the Hungarian
and Dominican interventions would have been forbidden had they
lacked U.N. authorization; similarly, in Vietnam, both the pro-
visions of arms by China and the provision of armed men by the
United States would also have been forbidden. In brief, in every
country it would be left to the people themselves to effect their
own political will through revolution, repression, or reform. Outside powers could not use military aid, a military presence, or military force to impose their own will.

Such a commitment would, of course, impose certain responsibilities upon the U.N. itself. In order to make its assertion of
authority real, it would have to provide observation and small-
scale enforcement units to seal off against military aid, invasion,
or infiltration the boundaries of a country in the midst of civil war.
Such a force ought to be present from the very beginning of the
danger, since illegal military intervention should be easier to prevent than to stop. If a revolution were to break out in Rumania, for

example, the immediate dispatch of mixed units of Poles, Egyptians, Indians, and Ghanaians would enormously increase the political risk and losses the Soviet Union would face by intervening, as it did in Hungary. Similarly, a small force of Swedes, Irishmen, Chileans, and Nigerians committed to resist intervention might have made the United States think twice before deciding to intervene in the Dominican Republic. Such a small-scale force ought to be available to the U.N. on extremely short notice—probably on a standby basis—and could perhaps be sent on the motion of the Secretary General whenever he found a condition of civil war to exist, subject to withdrawal of the force if neither the General Assembly nor the Security Council had upheld his action within ten days.

When would it be legitimate for the U.N. to authorize governments to intervene militarily in a civil war, or for the U.N. itself to support one side or the other? We believe that, so far as possible, the U.N. ought to restrict itself to intervening or permitting intervention only where there is very broad agreement among the real power units in the world that a great threat to the international peace is posed by one of the domestic contestants (or would be posed by those hostile to it in other countries, if that contestant won). Thus, if the rise of Hitler to power had resulted in a German civil war, and if a great majority of U.N. members (including all the great powers) had concluded that a victory by Hitler in that civil war posed a serious threat to world peace, the U.N. might have authorized Britain, France, and the Soviet Union to intervene, or have mounted a U.N. action. Or, if Rhodesia establishes her independence, a civil war erupts, and a pro-apartheid victory seems about to occur in such a way as to bring about international invasion first by the black African states and then by South Africa, resulting in a pan-African war, the U.N.—again only if supported by a majority—might authorize or carry out a military intervention on one side.

Now to the second sort of situation: military intervention in fear of a military threat. Just as it seems to us illegitimate to allow support for only one side in a civil war—either side—so it seems to us illegitimate to follow a double standard on this second kind of intervention. Intervention on Quemoy and Matsu by the Chinese in fear of an American military presence there is no more, or less, legitimate than intervention by the United States in or around Cuba to prevent the establishment of Soviet missile bases there. Both should be impossible unless first authorized by the U.N. as a necessary act of self-defense and as the lesser threat to international peace. But we must also understand that these acts of intervention were provoked by intense fear of a military threat, and in the real world, in the long run, if we are to prevent nations from taking similar actions in defense of what they believe to be their vital interests, the military threat would have to be abated. We would have to regard as "military intervention" the stationing of arms and armed men, and the provision of military aid, in foreign parts unless the U.N. had authorized it. In short, we would have to agree that all military alliances (except simple verbal agreements between nations to come to each other's defense) would have to be approved by the U.N. before going into force. Such an arrangement would in its turn depend on U.N. guarantees of the territorial integrity of weaker countries as against their stronger neighbors— and ultimately on very considerable measures of disarmament and the creation of sizable U.N. border-defense forces.

We therefore envisage a time-table something like this:

1. Immediate prohibition of military intervention inside the borders of a country involved in civil war.

2. Within a decade, prohibition of any military action to interfere with military arrangements made by two established governments where there was no civil war.

3. Within two decades, prohibition of any such "military arrangements," made even by two established governments, as would mean the international transfer of arms or armed men; and concomitant steps toward major disarmament.

II - *The Possibilities of Co-Operative Intervention*

Let us examine the implications of our general proposition that the forms of intervention now used by the United States must be reviewed and changed. We urge this in support of our view that even in support of noble ends, the United States may not use means that *would corrupt and destroy those ends*. Thus we do not believe that the use of saturation bombing, of napalm, of chemicals intended to destroy the rice crop, or of torture can be defended as necessary to the defense of liberty in Vietnam. Rather, we believe that such means *in fact* create chaos or totalitarian government, but never liberty. Therefore, not only should a system of international checks and balances through the U.N. be effected to end American military intervention and that of others in Vietnam; we ourselves, for the defense of our own values, should stop using military means that cannot advance liberty in such situations, and instead begin to use with great vigor and energy co-operative political and economic means.

Toward that end, we therefore urge the development of a whole new series of what might be thought of as the "unarmed forces" of the United States on the model of the Peace Corps, the Food for Peace Program, and the non-military programs of the Agency for International Development. Examples of such unarmed forces might be a Disaster Corps that would rebuild cities destroyed by earthquake or hurricane; a Conservation Corps that could irrigate and reforest the Sahara Desert; an Air Transport Force that would serve as a cargo and passenger service for developing countries that had not yet developed a rail or road network; an expanded Information Agency that could by radio and television help activate the politically suppressed or excluded and the economically desperate in countries like Paraguay, South Africa, or Albania—for example, broadcasting simple information on how to improve crop yields, on how to organize a political protest without risking lives, and on the outside world. Such unarmed forces should be closely attached to particular constituencies inside the United States, as the Peace Corps now is attached to the campus and Food for Peace to the farm. Thus the new unarmed forces might avoid both the abstract bureaucratism and the absence of vigorous domestic political support that have often afflicted the Agency for International Development.

As far as possible, the unarmed forces might use disarmed men and non-weapons material from those parts of the present

Armed Forces that could be dismantled as we abandoned military forms of intervention. But one thing should be clear: in proposing the development of these unarmed forces, we do not mean they should simply be "added on" to military intervention, as some semi-official strategists (from the Rand Corporation and elsewhere) have been proposing. We mean them to replace military intervention, and we would oppose any merger of counter-insurgency units, like the Special Forces and the CIA, with AID, Food for Peace, the Peace Corps, etc., in one great department for war-and-development, as some of the Rand proposals have suggested. We do not believe a "mix" of military and non-military forces can work in these situations. To use an inexact but suggestive analogy, such a "mix" would be the equivalent of SNCC's having entered Mississippi with a "mixture" of non-violence and murder. Suppose SNCC had spent only ten per cent of its time in carefully selected assassinations of those who resisted change or who called for the wrong kind of change? We believe that it would have utterly failed, and that Mississippi would now be in the throes of violence like that in Watts or Vietnam.

The focus of the unarmed forces should be what is now the great arena of conflict between mostly libertarian/democratic ways of organizing society and mostly totalitarian/autocratic ways —the arena of the non-industrial nations, in what has inaccurately but usefully been called the Southern Hemisphere: China, the rest of Asia (except for Japan), Africa, and Latin America. It is here, as those countries struggle their way toward technological society, that the way in which the struggle takes place, as well as whether it succeeds or fails, will determine whether new forms of free and democratic government or new forms of tyranny will emerge.

It is true that distinctions between liberty and tyranny are not easy for anyone outside a given society to make; what feels like my freedom to me may look like my subjection to someone from another country. When Americans attempt to help others to advance their own liberty, therefore, they should accept the others' definition of that liberty to the widest degree that can be squared with America's own conscientiously held values. For example, if the rulers of South Africa were to decide to define liberty for themselves as the extinction of all their African subjects, no one would argue that the United States should, at the South African government's request, supply economic aid in the form of gas ovens to effect the extinction. Indeed, in such a case the United States—or at least its private citizens—might well feel in conscience bound, for the sake of liberty, to offer food, money, radio-broadcasting and receiving equipment, and trained experts in non-violence to help Africans who decided to revolt against such a government. And if several such rebel groups requested help, one of which seemed very likely if it won to install totalitarian rules abolishing free speech, it would be wholly legitimate for the United States to withhold aid from that group while helping the others.

There are those who would argue that the only way the United States can advance liberty in the "Southern" world is to keep hands off, not even offering economic aid—or to offer such aid utterly "without strings." But no aid at all would condemn the Southern world either to permanent poverty or to a long nightmare of hyper-Stalinist capital accumulation, squeezing every drop of blood from peasants today so that their grandchildren can have a hydroelectric dam. And aid "without political strings" is simply a contradiction in terms: if aid goes to any government that requests it for any purpose, then its effect is to strengthen the political power of that government as against any internal opposition. If aid is conditioned upon an acceptable use of it, that of course means some strings are automatically attached: aid in the form of peace corpsmen for villages means that the villages are strengthened politically; aid in the form of training policemen means that the police and their commanders are strengthened politically, and so on. In any competition between different developed countries—the Soviet Union, the United States, France, etc.—over aid to the hungry nations, the aid itself is sure to reflect the deepest political presuppositions of each giver. In such a situation, therefore, the widest freedom of choice on the part of recipients will develop from a vigorous competition among the givers, rather than from subjection to a single source that can say "Take it or leave it" and thus impose its own strings.

For all these reasons, the United States need have no apologies about the vigorous program of development aid, so long as decisions as to what conditions to put on the aid are judged according to the particular country and situation, within the assumption that the aid is intended to help hungry nations develop in a democratic context, construed as broadly and generously as Americans can without breaking their own most basic standards of democracy. There might well be situations where the aid would be given, not to governments, but to opposition groups, and therefore might have to be smuggled in. The only absolute rule on all development aid would be that the sending of arms and armed men would be avoided, so that the United States would not again (as it has done in Vietnam) make the self-defeating and self-corrupting mistake of trying to deal with political conflicts by means of military suppression.

No one can spell out in detail the actions that would be needed to help bring about economic development in a context of democracy. Indeed, we need a great deal more research in how to help bring about the necessary changes in societies that are enormously different from each other. (Perhaps the undoubted talents of the Rand Corporation and other military "think tanks" could be redirected *in toto*, from the study of tenth-generation missile systems to the service of the unarmed forces.) Such research would need to answer questions like these: What forms of organization would allow a tribal society to make effective use of large amounts of American capital? Would it be wiser to bring Indians to the United States to study, or to create and give a full-fledged American school of agriculture to India, supplying the faculty until new Indians are trained for it and then continuing to pay the bills? Would Tuskegee Institute, Howard University, the Highlander Folk Center, or Swarthmore College be the best institution to provide teachers for Nigeria? What kinds of personality change might be necessary in key groups in a developing country in order to bring about development, and what actions would be likely to trigger such changes? What cheap new sources of energy might be developed which would allow villages to generate their own electricity instead of depending on an expensive national grid that would take years to build?

Although this research would undoubtedly lead to wholly new

approaches to development aid, some forms of aid now seem likely to be useful and should probably be greatly expanded:

1. Food-for-Peace aid to peasants who now are barely growing enough food to keep themselves alive, thus freeing them to work on development projects like dams, roads, and schools without damaging the international food market.

2. Use of certain industrial and military surpluses (tools, for example, and possibly whole moth-balled naval vessels that could be used as floating schools, hospitals, power generators, etc.).

3. Broadcasts of solid technical information on crops, carpentry, and similar problems over radio and television, combined with more political instruction on how to hold a village meeting democratically, etc.; plus free provision of battery-powered radio and television sets to millions of people in the non-industrial countries.

4. Most important of all, the provision of skilled and dedicated men of all sorts, in the various unarmed forces of the United States, to be prepared to cope with particular problems whenever they arise: in capitals that need trained administrators and planners to help train a new government in the techniques of long-range planning, democratic responsiveness to popular demands, etc.; in villages and urban slums that need people to teach irrigation or sanitation techniques or effective techniques of united civic or political action, etc.; in areas ruined by sudden natural disasters or by centuries of erosion and abuse that need people with the knowledge and machinery for reconstruction.

Undoubtedly, there would be some cases in which American energies would be insufficient to bring about an ascent into economic development within a democratic context. In short, there might be some defeats for liberty if the long war against poverty and tyranny were carried on by political and economic means; but it is hard to believe there would be anywhere near as many defeats as we have experienced in self-stultifying attempts to carry on that war by military means. And, in most cases, a vigorous effort by Americans to carry on the fight for liberty would "win"—not in the sense that Kenya, Brazil, or Burma would slavishly copy American institutions, but in the sense that they would be able to borrow, adapt, mix, and invent freely from the stock of ideas, approaches, and material goods that we and others could make available.

In all of this, we would insist on one major change in the American approach: that all our interventions on behalf of major social change in the underdeveloped world be carried on openly. It may be necessary to gather information by covert means; it is absolutely unnecessary, and indeed self-stultifying, to carry on "covert wars, covertly arrived at," as has on occasion been the American practice in Guatemala, Cuba, Indonesia, and a number of other places during the past fifteen years. Nor are covert wars the only illegitimate means. No covert operation, military or otherwise, can possibly be squared with, or be made to serve, the ends of democracy. Democratic government is peculiarly that form which requires public understanding, involvement, and criticism—and no intervention through secret bribery, blackmail, or assassination of political leaders can bring democratic government nearer in a country that does not have it. Indeed, the major effort of the unarmed forces should be to "activate" the excluded dispossessed, hopeless, angry, and apathetic of the world into a concern with shaping their own futures through political means that may not yet even exist and that could be invented from the fruitful meeting of young activators from America and men from totally different traditions. Such a function, like that of SNCC in Mississippi or SDS in the urban slums, would be public by its very nature.

III - The Construction of a World Forum

Let us examine, finally, our suggestion that many problems in the field of intervention could be dealt with more effectively if there were some way of focusing, legitimatizing, and institutionalizing the power of ideals and moral judgments in the world. To this point we have viewed the issue of intervention as one involving intense conflict between various national governments. We have avoided utopian notions of world community or human unity, in the belief that a realistic morality should work out ways of making conflict more creative—i.e., by making it a contest in "activating" rather than killing. But realistic morality could ignore the fact that there is a "growing edge" of values shared across national boundaries which does in fact point toward world community (and therefore, of course, to new kinds of conflict carried on along other than national lines). In the conflicts, "domestic" and "foreign," that trigger one or another kind of intervention and that would continue to do so in the sort of world we have pictured, it would be important for these new transnational values to be focused and for efforts to be made to find out what sorts of social changes the great majority of mankind would approve.

We propose, therefore, that the church and synagogue undertake—in a truly ecumenical spirit, going beyond the confines of present Christian or Judaeo-Christian ecumenism—to bring together for the constant review of world-conflict problems a permanent World Forum of what might be called the "value institutions" of mankind: the organizations of religious and philosophical reflection, the universities, the labor unions, the voluntary associations, the professional and scientific organizations, the social movements of moral and political renovation. This present National Inter-Religious Conference on Peace can itself be seen as a forerunner of such a World Forum, although of course as an American body it cannot reflect all the many currents of ideas in mankind. We believe that the conference should proceed toward the creation of a World Forum by involving progressively wider circles of institutions within and outside the United States. Ultimately, if it is to be truly representative of mankind, such a forum should include representatives, not only of the relatively voluntaristic, independent, and well-structured value institutions characteristic of most of the West and of the newer democratic nations, but of the relatively more centrally led and structured semi-private value institutions characteristic of more authoritarian societies, and also of the more fluid, more mercurial national and student movements characteristic of non-industrial societies undergoing revolutionary social change. Every effort should be made to invent ways of having such groups represented without descending, on the one hand, into the inclusion of self-appointed messiahs without followers, or, on the other, to the inclusion of institutions that are merely arms of the state. It may be, however, that the next stage of involvement to which this conference should address itself is the circle of institutions in the democratic world which are likely to be reasonably similar in structure to the sorts of institutions from which we at the conference come, though widely different in their values and assumptions.

Once constituted, the World Forum should make itself an independent center for the study of major conflict issues: should first gather and publish the facts in a given dispute and then, where it can, propose a remedy. It may be that in a surprising number of cases there would be wide agreement as to what should be done: about apartheid in South Africa, about the distribution of income in Brazil, about the war in Vietnam, about problems of liberty and authority in Ghana. Where, upon examination, such conflicts did, in fact, turn out to reflect some deep disagreement on solutions, the situation would be no worse than if it had never been studied. Even in such a case it might well be discovered that the division of opinion ran along other than national lines; and such a discovery would open possibilities of building new transnational lines.

The sort of role we are proposing for the churches and synagogues and their sister "value institutions" has already had an effect—however peripheral and scattered—on world politics. The new thought generated by *Pacem in Terris*, the slow-downs in the Vietnam war brought about in part through papal intervention— these have shown how the prestige of institutions without temporal power—*prestige based precisely on their lack of temporal power*— can be translated into another kind of power. Indeed, the effectiveness of Pope John XXIII and Pope Paul VI in acting for peace can be traced directly to the quality of their acts as "self-disestablishment" of the church, in the sense in which, at the beginning of this paper, we called for a new level and kind of disestablishment. For, where popes at one time in history would have accepted and welcomed the use of war by Christians to advance the power of the faith, Pope Paul today, by calling and working even-handedly for peace in Vietnam, has rejected precisely the notion that Christians can advance the faith by making war on atheists or infidels. He has in effect demanded that the state stop justifying the war on a religious basis, and in that way he has taken a new step in freeing the church from the suffocations of Establishment. A World Forum freely and independently studying conflict situations in the world, and working for peace by non-governmental action, would offer all the churches and synagogues and other value institutions the opportunity to do jointly what the Pope has so magnificently tried to do alone.

If the World Forum could gather the facts about a given conflict and could agree on a way to resolve the conflict, it might also be able to "intervene" in certain ways itself, to bring the conflict to an end. It could offer conciliation or mediation, it could supervise and certify elections, it could even—in an extreme situation of civil war, for example—provide men trained in non-violence who would interpose themselves between the parties, and all without any coercive power whatsoever, without any power but that of awakening the conscience of mankind.

We believe that the program we have offered for making "intervention" a creative, rather than a disastrous, act can be begun at once, as can the check-and-balance system for U.N. authorizations of military interventions in domestic civil wars; the developments of new American approaches to intervention through the medium to the unarmed forces; the creation of the World Forum, with whatever groups were prepared to join it. Of course, this program would not end here: the U.N. would need to be strengthened, the unarmed forces multiplied, the World Forum expanded. We have sketched a direction: what we have in mind is a world in which national governments continue for a considerable time to exist, but find their actions "surrounded" and moderated by international and transnational institutions. It is a world in which intervention is more likely to mean (but will not always mean) beneficial social change, rather than conquest or tyranny. It is a world sometimes of intense conflict and disagreement, sometimes of cooperation, but never or rarely of war. It is a world that seems to us attainable and desirable, conscious as we are both of man's capacity to build for evil and of his astonishing ability to use what he has built against itself, to create good.

2. Abridged Comments

Dean William E. Moran, Jr.

When the moralist undertakes to speak to the policy-maker, he must recognize that the policy-maker lives and acts in a real world, and that if he, as a moralist, refuses to face that real world or slides over difficult problems, he faces the risk of being treated as a kibitzer or a nuisance.

While the paper before us is entitled "Forms of Intervention: Moral Responsibilities and Limits," it treats primarily of violence and war rather than intervention. It offers no definition of intervention; nor does it seem opposed to interfering in the internal affairs of another country, whether with or without that country's consent. Indeed, it condones, even recommends, interference as long as it is not military in nature.

This construction implies that, despite the insistence in an early paragraph that no government may be allowed to judge in its own case, or to see itself as the redeemer of mankind, any government has the right to do so with other than military means. It would seem that the danger of exploitation and domination is as great here as in the case of military intervention. In this connection, I call attention to Pope John XXIII's *Mater et Magistra*, which reads as follows: "Moreover, economically developed countries should take particular care lest, in giving aid to poorer countries, they endeavor to turn the prevailing political situation to their own advantage, and seek to dominate." (par. 171)

Surely it is our responsibility to consider what constitutes intervention and those conditions in which it is morally acceptable, aside from the question of whether it is military in nature. There are worse things than violence: for us to stand by and watch the Chinese, in support of their national liberation movements, train people in exile, provide them with arms, infiltrate them back into their home country, provide them with volunteers as leaders, and create a civil war. To accept the fact that such things can and do happen in this world is to see the necessity for assuming our obligations wherever necessary.

Complementary to the above thought is the seeming unilateralism proposed in the paper. In the introductory portion, it speaks largely in universal terms. In its recommendations, it seems to make recommendations primarily, if not solely, to the United States. If this is a correct impression, I would suggest that it means that the United States—if it follows this advice—may render itself all pure and innocent and be unable to prevent the seizure of government by those who do not subscribe to Judaeo-Christian concepts concerning human dignity and freedom.

Throughout the paper it is suggested that, while any violent form of intervention should be condemned and forbidden, revolt by the oppressed and the suppressed should be promoted along non-violent lines. This raises a serious moral issue. Thus far, non-violence has proven a useful political tool in only a few countries with advanced democratic ideas; in India, for example, because the British were not prepared to shoot down masses of non-violent rioters. Yet, even there, there were occasions when it proved inadequate before independence was achieved, and particularly at the time of partition between India and Pakistan. So far, non-violence has proved effective in the United States; but when the Black Africans of South Africa made a peaceful protest at Sharpville, they were shot down. I hate to think what action the Russians would have taken if the Hungarian people, at the time of their revolt, had faced the Russian troops and tanks with masses in non-violent protest. Thus, unless we can be certain that any of the peoples who are oppressed could mount a successful non-violent revolution, it seems to me that we face the prospect of taking into our hands the lives of thousands, even hundreds of thousands, of other peoples.

In any consideration of the morality of various forms of intervention, thought should be given to the role of the U.N. in this regard, and how it could be improved so that it could play a larger role. And where the U.N. might consider its task primarily one of action, people of religious principles might consider theirs one of sifting facts, considering questions, and making recommendations, all toward the achievement of peace and the betterment of mankind.

Harold E. Stassen

One of the major new facts of the world in which we live is that modern implements of war are capable of the total destruction of mankind. Thus it seems crucial that we impose new and more effective moral restraints upon the use of military force throughout the world. In addition, we must seek new methods of settling issues and differences that in previous periods of history led to the use of military force in war.

The tremendous changes in science and technology which demand a keener sense of responsibility from mankind in general also have added relevance for man as an individual, with a deep and abiding faith in God and with a view that all of humanity are as children of one God, brothers and sisters within all of the nations of the world. As the worth and dignity of each person, of individual human rights and social responsibilities is recognized, so may be the need and value of a social, political, and economic system based on individual freedom and justice.

The foregoing basic approach leads me to a continuing opposition to communism and colonialism, to selfish economic exploitation, to self-centered social suppression, and to all political dictatorships. It also leads me to the belief that, in this modern age, any changes in these situations must be effected only by nonviolent means.

I must immediately emphasize, however, that the resort to military force by others may require the use of military force in defense, and that thorough preparation for such defense is one of the major deterrents against the use of military force by others. The principle of the necessity of moral restraint in the use of military force applies not only to an initial decision on its use, but also to the degree and continuity envisaged, even in cases of defense.

Thus, even where necessary, the use of military force must be so limited as to contribute toward the prevention of a war situation or, where one exists, to avoid expansion and escalation.

To me, this is where the new grim scientific and military facts of the nuclear age meet with the enduring moral principles of our religious faiths. It is the definition of this meeting ground which offers one of the most complex and significant areas for intelligent consideration at this time.

In taking up intervention specifically, it cannot be denied that the use of military force by the Communists presents a most difficult challenge. To fail to meet it could be to open the way toward the kind of world catastrophe, multiplied many times, that occurred when the world failed to meet the early military thrusts of Hitler.

On the other hand, to meet this challenge without moral restraint, without the most intelligent care, could be the destruction of the very moral fabric upon which the future of civilization must depend.

I salute and honor the American military men who, even as I speak, are endeavoring to carry out their present orders in Vietnam. I believe that so long as they are under those orders, they should be supported with all the necessary equipment, supplies, and funds. But let me also state that I believe the highest acts of patriotism within the United States will be those of persuading the President to replace those orders with directions toward the attainment of peace for all the people of Vietnam.

Even as I speak with feeling of the depths of the mistake that has been made, I understand full well the basis on which it was made. I have seen over and over again the sincere urgings to solve problems by American military means, the tempting alternative that was put before President Eisenhower in the Philippine situation with the Communist Huk guerrillas, at the time of Hungarian fighting, and when Guatemala was under a Communist government; before President Kennedy in the Cuban situation; before President Truman at the time of the Berlin blockade. I believe that all humanity can be thankful that in these instances the principles of moral restraint came through and the United States did not initiate war action.

In most of these cases the firm but patient, persistent building for peace against communism has proved its rightness and success. I believe that in the future the freedom of the people of Cuba and Hungary will be re-established, and by non-military means. I am equally convinced that the hasty use of direct American combat forces in war action would have had a tragic result.

I have a deep faith and confident optimism that if we think through the principles of moral restraint and moral responsibility, and if we interpret them with persistence and patience, there can be a future of peace, with freedom and justice throughout the world. Let us work toward the establishment of that which will make it possible for all peoples everywhere to achieve freedom from exploitation and suppression by non-violent means.

Dr. Gordon C. Zahn

It is not often that a religious pacifist has the opportunity to comment upon a paper that offers him such broad scope for enthusiastic agreement. There are several features which deserve special praise. Certainly the most significant note is the firm statement that, as "men of God and men of liberty," we are prepared to tell the secular magistrates that "we will advance our values and our visions, by using our means of spiritual appeal; that we do not need and do not want the state to advance our values at the point of a gun or the drop of a bomb." If we can persist in that principle and implement it in the actions we take here, we will have won for all the engaged religious communities a new and necessary range of free movement and will have made it difficult, if not impossible, for the magistrates of power to do what they have so often succeeded in doing in the past—that is, to "capture" the religious community and reduce it to an instrument serving their own purposes. In this connection, I am thinking of recent statements made by some of our own national spokesmen ostensibly "welcoming" and "supporting" the peace-oriented ventures of religious leaders like Pope Paul VI—at the same time that they announce new escalations of conflict that are clearly opposed to the spirit, and often enough the content, of those same appeals. What we have in this paper is a declaration of independence which will bring about a new kind of "separation of church and state," making it harder for national leaders to clothe their actions in the convenient mantle of high-sounding but empty pieties.

It is all too easy, when we engage in discussions of these matters, to lose focus and permit the argument to stray too far afield into areas in which our competence as religionists and believers might be dismissed. For this reason it is of utmost importance that our criticisms and proposals concerning national policy always be held firmly in the context of the moral principles that are involved and that, we must insist, always take priority over temporal dimensions and considerations, even those bearing upon what may seem to be the "imperatives" of national security and national prestige. We speak here for religion and its values; we do not speak as political, diplomatic, or military experts. But let us not be in the least defensive when making this admission. Instead, let us make it clear that our area of "expertise," if you will, is and should be recognized as being by far the most important, if the welfare of mankind is to be taken into account. I would suggest, therefore, that the moral principles stated in an early paragraph be linked as specifically as possible with each of the proposals which follow in the text.

It is unquestionably an accomplishment to produce a statement of principles that we hope will perform an educative function for the population at large and have some influence upon those who direct our nation's policies. I question whether this is enough. Taking the 1963 National Conference on Race and Religion as a model of what we might hope to accomplish here, I would hold that the real accomplishment of that gathering was the inspiration and organization of effective action by committed individuals as an expression of their personal responsibility. In this regard, I feel that this paper fails to move the issue from the level of broad national policy to that of individual obligation—and the religious communities' responsibility to awaken their members to those obligations.

What this document lacks is something that was attempted (with only partial success) in the writing of the Vatican Council's schema on "The Church in the Modern World." The religious communities should put themselves firmly "on record" as being prepared to accord a greater measure of respect and encouragement to those members who reject the ways of violence and who refuse to support interventions that rest upon the use of violence.

By the same token, the religious communities should be prepared to function as a source of such civil dissent and even disobedience when policies leading to military interventions or other interventions that go beyond the limits set by the Judaeo-Christian religious traditions are contemplated or actually initiated by a nation. It is an irony of history that even those religious communities that have a relatively detailed "theology of the just war" never seem to get around to applying its principles and conditions to either actual or threatened wars. This, I feel, must be changed if our voice is to be heard at all; and I would like to see this conference give some consideration to ways in which this change can be effected.

A possible form of intervention seems to have been overlooked —the recourse, on the part of an activated membership, to those "weapons of the spirit" that should serve as the most appropriate channel of the churches' influence upon human affairs. I mention this only in passing (and with some hesitance, I confess). It is not so much that I fear participants in a conference like this will shrug this aside as too idealistic or irrelevant; rather, I see a danger that some will be all too willing to substitute a total reliance upon such things as prayer and fasting for the type of activities proposed by the authors of our paper. Needless to say, such a switch is not contemplated in my raising the issue at this point.

Just as the success of a military intervention depends in great measure upon the depth of commitment that can be created in the individual fighting man, so, I feel, must we incorporate a similar concern for the depth of commitment we can and must win from those who will be called upon to carry the burden of the kind of interventions we propose. And even if we prefer to keep the focus at the broader level of official national policies and the influence the religious communities can have upon them, our efforts will be successful only to the degree that we demonstrate that the religious communities "mean business," that they are prepared to support only those forms of intervention which meet the moral responsibilities and limits we seek to set, and—perhaps even more important —that they are also prepared to oppose all forms of intervention which do not.

APPENDIX B

Officers and Participants

SECRETARIAT

Rabbi Balfour Brickner, Rev. Leonidas C. Contos, Rev. Clifford Earle, Rev. John H. Eberly, Mr. James Finn, Dr. Alan F. Geyer, Rev. Herschel Halbert, Dr. Homer A. Jack, Mr. Herman Will, Jr., and Dr. E. Raymond Wilson.

ADMINISTRATIVE SECRETARY

Mrs. Kay Shannon

PARTICIPANTS*

Rabbi A. Nathan Abramowitz, Washington, D.C.

Rabbi Jacob Agus, Baltimore, Md.

Mathew Ahmann, Chicago, Ill.

Vivodh ZH Anand, Bloomfield, N.J.

Hugh Anwyl, Los Angeles, Cal.

David Banks, Louisville, Ky.

Mrs. Paul J. Basinger, Chicago, Ill.

Charles S. Beal, Winnetka, Ill.

E. Edward Behre, Philadelphia, Pa.

Rt. Rev. Msgr. A. W. Behrens, Washington, D.C.

Colin W. Bell, Philadelphia, Pa.

Mrs. Harold W. Bell, Jr., Laguna Beach, Cal.

Dr. and Mrs. John C. Bennett, New York, N.Y.

Rabbi Saul P. Besser, Washington, D.C.

Rev. Donald Black, New York, N.Y.

Mrs. Werner J. Blanchard, Dayton, Ohio

Prof. Eugene Boardman, Washington, D.C.

Rev. David J. Bort, Orange, N.J.

Dr. Harold A. Bosley, New York, N.Y.

Rev. John F. Bowyer, Mannington, W. Va.

Rabbi Joseph M. Brandriss, Silver Spring, Md.

Rabbi Balfour Brickner, New York, N.Y.

Rabbi Herbert Bronstein, Rochester, N.Y.

Mr. and Mrs. Frederick Brooks, Davis, Cal.

* Each registered participant has been asked whether he or she would like to be listed in this volume. Only those who replied are listed, a fact that does not automatically imply concurrence with the Conference Declaration or endorsement of the three workshop reports.

Dr. Robert D. Bulkley, Philadelphia, Pa.
Bishop Henry C. Bunton, Washington, D.C.
Rev. E. James Caldwell, Erie, Pa.
Mrs. John W. Carroll, Swarthmore, Pa.
William Chafets, New York, N.Y.
Mrs. Theodore S. Chapman, Hinsdale, Ill.
Rev. James A. Clark, Washington, D.C.
Miss Caren A. Cogswell, Alexandria, Va.
Rev. David H. Cole, Rockville, Md.
Rev. Louis M. Colonnese, Davenport, Iowa
Rev. Leonides C. Contos, New York, N.Y.
Frank L. Cooley, Ithaca, N.Y.
Marvin Cooper, Miami Beach, Fla.
Rev. Jack Corbett, Washington, D.C.
James Couchell, New York, N.Y.
Rt. Rev. and Mrs. William Crittenden, Erie, Pa.
Rt. Rev. William Davidson, Salina, Kan.
Rev. Gardiner M. Day, Cambridge, Mass.
Dean L. Harold DeWolf, Washington, D.C.
Sister M. Mildred Dolores, Washington, D.C.
George R. Donahue, New York, N.Y.
Rev. M. Everett Dorr, Fairfax, Va.
Rev. William K. DuVal, New York, N.Y.
John H. Eberly, Washington, D.C.
Rabbi Maurice N. Eisendrath, New York, N.Y.
Mrs. Lewis A. Eldridge, Rensselaerville, N.Y.
Miss Jane Evans, New York, N.Y.
Irving Jay Fain, Providence, R.I.
Robert A. Fangmeier, Indianapolis, Ind.
Donald A. Farrell, Washington, D.C.
Mrs. Joe S. Faulconer, Ashland, Ky.
Dr. Vernon Ferwerda, Washington, D.C.
James Finn, New York, N.Y.
James H. Forest, New York, N.Y.
Peter Forsythe, Ann Arbor, Mich.
Sister Mary Francisca, Maryknoll, N.Y.
Mrs. Harold G. Freund, Blue Springs, Mo.
Mrs. Albert Fried, Brooklyn, N.Y.
Dr. Henri Front, Philadelphia, Pa.

Mrs. Russell M. Fuller, Ann Arbor, Mich.
Sister M. Gabriella, Framingham, Mass.
James Gallagher, New York, N.Y.
Dr. Harry M. Gardner, Arlington, Va.
Stephen Garfinkel, Wanamasee, N.J.
Dr. Alan F. Geyer, New York, N.Y.
Rev. H. Lamar Gibble, Kensington, Md.
Rabbi Arthur Gilbert, New York, N.Y.
Rev. David A. Giles, New York, N.Y.
Dr. Robert W. Gilmore, New York, N.Y.
Rabbi Roland B. Gittelsohn, Chestnut Hill, Mass.
Rabbi Joseph B. Glaser, San Francisco, Cal.
Bishop Charles F. Golden, Nashville, Tenn.
Rabbi Theodore Gordon, Wynnewood, Pa.
Mrs. William A. Gordon, Noroton, Conn.
Mrs. Jo Kreiner Graham, Philadelphia, Pa.
Dr. Dana McLean Greeley, Boston, Mass.
Rev. Herschel Halbert, New York, N.Y.
Prof. Robert W. Hallgring, Seattle, Wash.
George C. Hardin, Philadelphia, Pa.
Rev. Thomas Lee Hayes, Gibsonia, Pa.
Robert Heath, Washington, D.C.
Rev. John C. Heidbrink, Nyack, N.Y.
Rev. Cletus E. Hirschy, Washington, D.C.
Nathaniel E. Hess, Sands Point, N.Y.
Dieter T. Hessel, Philadelphia, Pa.
Rt. Rev. Msgr. George C. Higgins, Washington, D.C.
Rev. George G. Hill, Hartford, Conn.
William Chris Hobgood, Alexandria, Va.
Eric Hoffman, New York, N.Y.
Prof. Arthur N. Holcombe, Philadelphia, Pa.
Mrs. Cecile S. Holley, Washington, D.C.
Rev. Robert W. Hovda, Washington, D.C.
Rev. Ora I. Huston, Elgin, Ill.
E. W. Hymer, New York, N.Y.
Ralph Douglas Hyslop, New York, N.Y.
Sister M. Jacqueline, Framingham, Mass.
Rabbi Sanford Jarashow, Chevy Chase, Md.
Robert E. Jones, Washington, D.C.
Rabbi Arnold G. Kaiman, Huntingdon Valley, Pa.

Dr. Max A. Kapp, Boston, Mass.
Sidney R. Katz, New York, N.Y.
Robert Katzoff, Baltimore, Md.
Rev. Robert Kellerman, Binghamton, N.Y.
Charles J. Kelly, Washington, D.C.
Frank K. Kelly, Santa Barbara, Cal.
Miss Elmira Kendricks, New York, N.Y.
Dumont F. Kenny, West Cornwall, Conn.
Rabbi Stanley Kessler, West Hartford, Conn.
Rev. William W. Keys, II, Bethesda, Md.
Rev. Paul R. Killinger, Orange, Cal.
Mrs. Charles Kinney, New Britain, Conn.
Rev. Daisuke Kitagawa, New York, N.Y.
Rabbi Leon Kronish, Miami Beach, Fla.
Rev. Mrs. Harriet B. Kurtz, Chappaqua, N.Y.
Cardinal J. Landes, Franklin, Ohio
Glenn S. Larson, Beverly, Mass.
Morris Laub, New York, N.Y.
Gunther Lawrence, New York, N.Y.
Sylvan Lebow, New York, N.Y.
Rabbi Arthur Lelyveld, Cleveland, Ohio
Rabbi Eugene J. Lipman, Washington, D.C.
Clark Lobenstine, Annapolis, Md.
Bishop John Wesley Lord, Washington, D.C.
Sidney Lovett, Jr., Arlington, Va.
Frank C. Mabee, Enid, Okla.
L. D. MacIntyre, Bethesda, Md.
Mrs. Freda Magid, Los Angeles, Cal.
Robert Mang, San Francisco, Cal.
Rabbi Robert J. Marx, Chicago, Ill.
Rev. John E. Mayne, Arlington, Va.
John P. C. Matthews, Princeton, N.J.
Rev. Donald W. McIlvane, Pittsburgh, Pa.
Rev. W. J. H. McKnight, New York, N.Y.
Rev. John H. McMahon, Monroeville, Pa.
Stewart Meacham, Philadelphia, Pa.
Rev. and Mrs. Harry C. Meserve, Grosse Pointe, Mich.
Rev. James L. Meyer, Washington, D.C.
Gerald F. Mische, Paterson, N.J.
Dean and Mrs. William E. Moran, Jr., Washington, D.C.

Msgr. Edward G. Murray, Boston, Mass.
Rev. Albert P. Neilson, Wilmington, Del.
Rev. Carl J. Nelson, Eugene, Oregon
Rev. Claud D. Nelson, New York, N.Y.
Dr. F. Burton Nelson, Chicago, Ill.
Rev. Richard John Neuhaus, Brooklyn, N.Y.
Mrs. Mary-Cushing Niles, Baltimore, Md.
Rudolph F. J. Nobis, North Canton, Ohio
John Allen O'Connor, Wilmington, Del.
Msgr. John H. Oesterreicher, Seton Hall, N.J.
C. Arild Olsen, New York, N.Y.
Rev. Arnold O. Olson, Poughkeepsie, N.Y.
Mrs. Jean P. Patterson, San Jose, Costa Rica
Dr. Paul Peachey, Washington, D.C.
Dr. Sarah M. Pereira, Washington, D.C.
Rabbi Hayim Goren Perelmuter, Chicago, Ill.
Allison W. Phinney, Jr., Boston, Mass.
Rabbi Ely E. Pilchik, South Orange, N.J.
Rev. Robert Pollard III, Valley Cottage, N.Y.
Mrs. Elizabeth H. Polster, Southampton, Pa.
Rev. William G. Poole, Paintsville, Ky.
Thomas E. Quigley, Washington, D.C.
Rabbi Stanley Rabinowitz, Washington, D. C.
Dr. Darrell Randall, Washington, D.C.
Miss Dorothy J. Rasenberger, Loveland, Ohio
Rabbi Sidney L. Regner, New York, N.Y.
Rabbi Michael A. Robinson, Croton-on-Hudson, N.Y.
Alfred Ronald, Passaic, N.J.
John D. Roop, Elgin, Ill.
Rev. Charles Rother, Washington, D.C.
Dr. W. Harold Row, Elgin, Ill.
Howard E. Royer, Elgin, Ill.
Rabbi Byron T. Rubenstein, Westport, Conn.
Wade D. Rubick, Indianapolis, Ind.
Mrs. Merryle S. Rukeyser, New Rochelle, N.Y.
Patricia Rusk, New York, N.Y.
Mr. and Mrs. Kenneth Russ, Wilmette, Ill.
Rev. John Nevin Sayre, Nyack, N.Y.
Judith E. Schatz, New York, N.Y.
Rev. Werner-Christoph Schmauch, New York, N.Y.

Dr. Howard Schomer, Chicago, Ill.
Rev. Joseph Schubert, Washington, D.C.
Ben Seaver, San Francisco, Cal.
Dr. Simon Segal, New York, N.Y.
George A. Selleck, Cambridge, Mass.
Mrs. Kay Shannon, Washington, D.C.
Father Mario William Shaw, Indianapolis, Ind.
Rev. Rodney Shaw, Washington, D.C.
Rev. John B. Sheerin, New York, N.Y.
Mrs. Horace A. Shonle, Indianapolis, Ind.
Rev. Ralph E. Smeltzer, Elgin, Ill.
Edward F. Snyder, Washington, D.C.
Rabbi Samuel D. Soskin, Brooklyn, N.Y.
Dr. Carl Soule, New York, N.Y.
Mr. and Mrs. Frank Speltz, Washington, D.C.
Howard Spessard, Hagerstown, Md.
Mrs. Leonard Spring, New York, N.Y.
Mrs. Warren L. Starrett, Erie, Pa.
Harold E. Stassen, Philadelphia, Pa.
Rev. Robert P. Stenger, Dubuque, Iowa
Dr. J. Buroughs Stokes, Washington, D.C.
Rev. and Mrs. Robbins Strong, New York, N.Y.
Edward Sypulski, Beauty, Ky.
Mrs. Max F. Thompson, Boston, Mass.
Cornelius C. Tarplee, New York, N.Y.
Rev. Alexander Veronis, Lancaster, Pa.
Albert Vorspan, New York, N.Y.
Rabbi Harold Waintrup, Abington, Pa.
Dr. A. Dudley Ward, Washington, D.C.
Dr. Arthur I. Waskow, Washington, D.C.
Rabbi Jacob J. Weinstein, Chicago, Ill.
Gerard N. T. Widdrington, New York, N.Y.
E. Raymond Wilson, Washington, D.C.
Rev. Alfred R. Winham, Jackson, Miss.
Bishop John J. Wright, Pittsburgh, Pa.
Rt. Rev. Thomas H. Wright, Wilmington, N.D.
John H. Yoder, Elkhart, Ind.
Ronald J. Young, Nyack, N.Y.
Dr. Gordon Zahn, Chicago, Ill.
Dr. Nevin H. Zuck, Elizabethtown, Pa.

APPENDIX C

Partial List of Peace Organizations[*]

General

Ad Hoc Committee on the Human Rights and Genocide Treaties, 25 E. 78th St., New York, N.Y. 10021.

American Committee on Africa, 211 E. 43rd St., New York, N.Y. 10017.

Carnegie Endowment for International Peace, 335 E. 46th St., New York, N.Y. 10017.

Center for the Study of Democratic Institutions, Box 4068, Santa Barbara, Cal. 93103.

Central Committee for Conscientious Objectors, 2006 Walnut St., Philadelphia, Pa. 19103.

Committee for Non-Violent Action, 325 Lafayette St., New York, N.Y. 10012.

Committee for World Development and World Disarmament, 218 E. 18th St., New York, N.Y. 10003.

Council for a Livable World, 1346 Connecticut Ave. N.W., Washington, D.C. 20036.

Council on Foreign Relations, 58 E. 68th St., New York, N.Y. 10021.

Foreign Policy Association, 345 E. 46th St., New York, N.Y. 10017.

---

[*] This is an incomplete list of U.S. peace organizations, many of which, however, were informally represented at the National Inter-Religious Conference on Peace.

International League for the Rights of Man, 156 Fifth Ave., New York, N.Y. 10010.
National Committee for a Sane Nuclear Policy, 17 E. 45th St., New York, N.Y. 10017.
National Service Board for Religious Objectors, 15th and New York Ave. N.W., Washington, D.C. 20005.
Turn Toward Peace, 218 E. 18th St., New York, N.Y. 10003.
United Nations Association, 345 E. 46th St., New York, N.Y. 10017.
United World Federalists, 1346 Connecticut Ave. N.W., Washington, D.C. 20036.
War Resisters League, 5 Beekman St., New York, N.Y. 10038.
Women's International League for Peace and Freedom, 2006 Walnut St., Philadelphia, Pa. 19103.

Religion and Peace (Official)

American Baptist Convention, Division of Christian Social Concern, Valley Forge, Pa.
American Ethical Union, 2 W. 64th St., New York, N.Y. 10023.
Church of the Brethren Service Commission, 1451 Dundee Ave., Elgin, Ill. 60120.
Christian Churches (Disciples of Christ), Christian Action and Community Services, 221 Ohmer Ave., Indianapolis 19, Ind.
Episcopal Church, Dept. of Christian Social Relations, 815 Second Ave., New York, N.Y. 10017.
Friends Peace Committee, 1520 Race St., Philadelphia, Pa.
Eastern Orthodox Catholic Church in America, 777 U.N. Plaza, New York, N.Y. 10017.
Mennonite Central Committee, 21 S. 12th St., Akron, Pa.
The Methodist Church, Board of Christian Social Concerns, 100 Maryland Ave. N.E., Washington, D.C. 20002.
National Catholic Welfare Conference, 1312 Massachusetts Ave. N.W., Washington, D.C. 20005.
National Council of Churches, Dept. of International Affairs, 475 Riverside Drive, New York, N.Y. 10027.
National Lutheran Council, 50 Madison Ave., New York, N.Y. 10010.
Presbyterian Church in the U.S., P.O. Box 1176, Richmond, Va. 23209.

Union of American Hebrew Congregations, Commission on Social Action, 838 Fifth Ave., New York, N.Y. 10021.

Unitarian Universalist Association, Dept. of Social Responsibility, 25 Beacon St., Boston, Mass. 02108.

United Church of Christ, Council on Christian Social Action, 777 U.N. Plaza, New York, N.Y. 10017.

United Presbyterian Church in the U.S., Office of Church and Society, Witherspoon Bldg., Philadelphia, Pa. 19107.

World Council of Churches, Commission of the Churches on International Affairs, 297 Park Ave. South, New York, N.Y. 10010.

Religion and Peace (Unofficial)

American Friends Service Committee, 160 N. 15th St., Philadelphia, Pa.

American Pax Association, Box 139, Murry Hill Station, New York, N.Y. 10016.

Baptist Peace Fellowship, Valley Forge, Pa.

Catholic Association for International Peace, 1312 Massachusetts Ave. N.W., Washington, D.C. 20005.

Catholic Peace Fellowship, 5 Beekman St., New York, N.Y. 10038.

Catholic Worker, 175 Chrystie St., New York, N.Y. 10002.

Church Peace Mission, 4102 Brandywine St. N.W., Washington, D.C. 20016.

Conference on Christian Approaches to Defense and Disarmament, Room 9D, 777 U.N. Plaza, New York, N.Y. 10017.

Council on Religion and International Affairs, 170 E. 64th St., New York, N.Y. 10021.

Disciples Peace Fellowship, 222 S. Downey Ave., Indianapolis, Ind.

Episcopal Peace Fellowship, Christ Church, 229 E. 59th St., New York, N.Y. 10022.

Fellowship of Ethical Pacifists, c/o Friedlander, 382 Central Park West, New York, N.Y. 10025.

Methodist Peace Fellowship, c/o Terry, Old Rock Hill Road, Wallingford, Conn. 06492.

Fellowship of Reconciliation, Box 271, Nyack, N.Y. 10960.

Friends Committee on National Legislation, 245 Second St. N.E., Washington, D.C. 20002.

Inter-Religious Committee on Peace, 25 Beacon St., Boston, Mass. 02108.

Jewish Peace Fellowship, c/o Robinson, Glengary Road, Croton-on-Hudson, N.Y.

Liberal Religious Peace Fellowship, c/o Underwood, 1 Lafayette Plaisance, Apt. 802, Detroit, Mich. 48207.

Lutheran Peace Fellowship, c/o Hawkinson, 1605 E. River Road, Minneapolis, Minn. 55414.

National Emergency Committee of Clergy Concerned about Vietnam, 475 Riverside Drive, New York, N.Y. 10027.

National Conference of Christians and Jews, 43 W. 57th St., New York, N.Y. 10019.

New Church Pacifist Fellowship, c/o Bischof, 108 Garfield St., Garden City, N.Y.

Reformed Church Peace Fellowship, c/o Jenks, East Church Street, Spring Valley, N.Y.

Southern Presbyterian Peace Fellowship, c/o Lofquist, 1411 Anderson St., Wilson, N.C.

United Church Peace Fellowship, c/o Braun, 21 Forest Ave., Glen Ridge, N.J.

United Presbyterian Peace Fellowship, Box 325, Bound Brook, N.J.

United States Committee for the Christian Peace Conference, c/o Prof. Charles C. West, Princeton Theological Seminary, Princeton, N.J.

APPENDIX D

Biographies of Contributors

SALVATORE ADAMO is executive editor of *The Catholic Star Herald* of Camden, N.J.

ARTHUR W. BARBER is Deputy Assistant Secretary of Defense for International Security Affairs. A graduate in physics of Harvard University, Mr. Barber has been a physicist for the U.S. Air Force and the Mitre Corporation.

JOHN C. BENNETT is President of Union Theological Seminary. A minister in the United Church of Christ, Dr. Bennett has been on the faculty of Union Theological Seminary since 1943. He is the author of many volumes, including *Social Salvation* (1935), *Christian Ethics and Social Policy* (1946), and *Christians and the State* (1958).

HUBERT H. HUMPHREY is Vice President of the United States.

HOMER A. JACK is Director of the Department of Social Responsibility of the Unitarian Universalist Association (of the United States and Canada). A Unitarian Universalist minister, Dr. Jack was chairman of the secretariat of the National Inter-Religious Conference on Peace.

LYNDON B. JOHNSON is President of the United States.

ARTHUR MOORE is editor of *World Outlook*, a Methodist periodical.

STEVEN S. SCHWARZSCHILD is associate professor of philosophy at Washington University and editor of *Judaism, A Quarterly Journal.*

U THANT is Secretary General of the United Nations.

JACOB J. WEINSTEIN is President of the Central Conference of American Rabbis. Rabbi Weinstein has been spiritual leader of K.A.M. Temple in Chicago since 1939.

JOHN J. WRIGHT is Bishop of the Pittsburgh Diocese of the Catholic Church. Formerly Bishop of Worcester, Mass., Bishop Wright was a member of the Theological Commission of Vatican Council II. He is author of several volumes, including *National Patriotism in Papal Teaching* (1939), and *The Pope and the War* (1944).